According to Latest NEP Syllabus

Fundamentals of Information Technology and Computer Applications

[For Information Technology and Computer Application 1st Semester students]

By

Dr. Wasim Akram Zargar

Head Deptt. Of Information Technology

Govt. Degree College, Sopore

PREFACE

The Present book of Information Technology is meant for Information Technology and Computer Application 1st Semester students. The book has been written strictly according to the latest NEP syllabus and contains whole subject matter required by the syllabus.

The syllabus has been divided into five chapters namely Information Technology and Computers, Input Output Devices and Memory, Computer Software and Languages, Networking and IT Trends, Number System and Data Information Concept.

This book has been written in simple language explaining basic concepts with explanation, diagrams and examples where found necessary.

I hope that the book on its present form will be beneficial for readers (students and professors). The comments and suggestions for further improvement of the book are cordially invited.

Dr. Wasim Akram Zargar

Contents

Chapter 1: Information Technology and Computers

Data:

Data is raw material, unorganized facts used as input that need to be processed. Data can be something simple and random and useless until it is organized.

Information:

When data is processed, organized or presented in a given context so as to make it useful i: e; output, it is called information.

Information processing:

Information processing refers to the manipulation of digitized information by computers and other digital electronic equipment, known collectively as information technology (IT). Information processing systems include business software, operating systems, computers, networks and mainframes. Whenever data needs to be transferred or operated upon in some way, this is referred to as information processing.

Characteristics of Information:

The parameters of a good quality are difficult to determine for information. Quality of information refers to its fitness for use, or its reliability. Following are the essential characteristic features:

I. **Timeliness:** Timeliness means that information must reach the recipients within the prescribed timeframes. For effective decision making, information must reach the decision-maker at the right time, i.e., recipients must get information when they need it. Delays destroys the value of information. The characteristic of timeliness, to be effective, should also include up-to-date, i.e., current information.

II. **Accuracy:** Information should be accurate. It means that information should be free from mistakes, errors &, clear. Accuracy also means that the information is free from bias. Wrong information given to management would result in wrong decisions. As managers decisions are based on the information supplied in MIS reports, all managers need accurate information.

III. **Relevance:** Information is said to be relevant if it answers especially for the recipient what, why, where, when, who and why? In other words, the MIS should serve reports to managers which is useful and the information helps them to make decisions.

IV. **Adequacy:** Adequacy means information must be sufficient in quantity, i.e., MIS must provide reports containing information which is required in the deciding processes of decision-making. The report should not give inadequate or for that matter, more than adequate information, which may create a difficult situation for the decision-maker. Whereas inadequacy of information leads to crises, information overload results in chaos.

V. **Completeness:** The information which is given to a manager must be complete and should meet all his needs. Incomplete information may result in wrong decisions and thus may prove costly to the organization.

VI. **Explicitness:** A report is said to be of good quality if it does not require further analysis by the recipients for decision making.

VII.   **Impartiality:** Impartial information contains no bias and has been collected without any distorted view of the situation.

Information system:

Information system (IS) refers to a collection of multiple pieces of equipment involved in the dissemination of information. Hardware, software, computer system connections and information, information system users, and the system's housing are all part of an IS. There are several types of information systems, including the following common types:

i.   Operations support systems, including transaction processing systems.
ii.   Management information systems.
iii.   Decision support systems.
iv.   Executive information systems

An information system commonly refers to a basic computer system but may also describe a telephone switching or environmental controlling system. The IS involves resources for shared or processed information, as well as the people who manage the system. People are considered part of the system because without them, systems would not operate correctly. There are many types of information systems, depending on the need they are designed to fill. An operations support system, such as a transaction processing system, converts business data (financial transactions) into valuable information. Similarly, a management information system uses database information to output reports, helping users and businesses make decisions based on extracted data.

Information Technology:

The technology involving the improvement, protection, maintenance, and use of computer systems, software, and networks for the processing and distribution of data. Information technology refers to something associated with computing technology, which includes networking, hardware, software, the Internet, or the people that work with this technology. Many corporations now have IT departments for dealing with the computer systems, networks, and different technical regions of their companies. IT jobs consist of computer programming, network management, computer engineering, Web improvement, technical assist, and plenty of different related occupations. Since we stay inside the " information age," IT has become a part of our ordinary lives.

Computer:

A computer may be defined as a machine that can solve problems at high speed by accepting data as input, performing certain operations and presenting the results as output of those operations. These operations performed by a set of sequenced instructions called program. A computer can store, process and retrieve data wherever needed due to these functions it is also known as Data processor.

Full form of Computer is

C - commonly
O - operation
M - machine
P - particularly
U - used for
T - technical

E - educational

R - research.

Block Diagram of Computer System:

The computer system consists of mainly three types that are central processing unit (CPU), Input Devices, and Output Devices. The Central processing unit (CPU) again consists of ALU (Arithmetic Logic Unit) and Control Unit. The set of instruction is presented to the computer in the form of raw data which is entered through input devices such as keyboard or mouse.

Later this set of instruction is processed with the help of CPU, and the computer system Produce an Output with the help of Output Devices mainly Printers and monitors. Large amount of data is stored in the computer memory with the help of primary and secondary storage devices temporarily and permanently. This are called as storage devices

The CPU is the heart | Brian of a computer because without the necessary action taken by the CPU the user cannot get the desired output. The central Processing unit [CPU] is responsible for processing all the Instruction which is given to computer system or PC. Below Block Diagram of Computer and Its Components are mentioned for Better Understanding

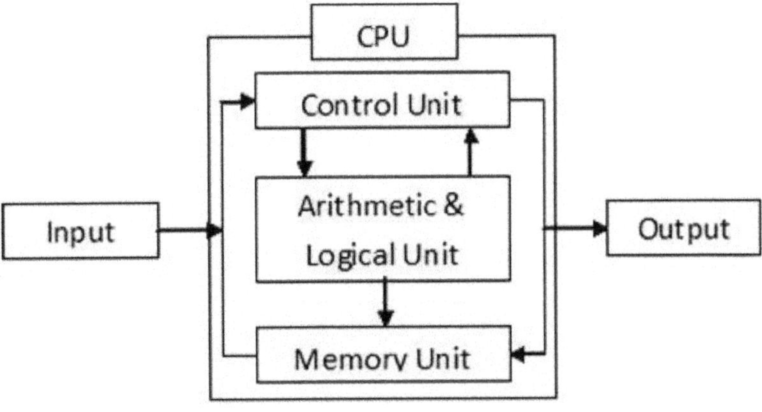

Fig. Block Diagram of Computer

Input Devices: The set of instruction or information is provided to the computer system or PC with the help of input devices such as (keyboard, mouse, scanners etc.). The Instruction or data presented to computer system is converted into binary form then it is supplied to computer system for further processing. The Input devices enters the data from outside the world into the primary storage devices. The input devices are a means of communication with outside world and our computer system.

Output devices: Output devices of computer produce or generate results with the help of devices or gadgets such as printer, monitor etc. primarily these instruction or data provided to computer system is in binary code so to produce or generate the desired output the system has to convert this data into human-readable form, to do so it has to first present the data or instruction to computer system for further processing or handling. With the help and assistance of output devices, the system is linked or connected with outside world. For Example, the data or instruction such as Graphics, images or text is inserted in the computer system with the help of input devices as the data received from the input devices is in binary code, therefore, the data has to be primarily converted into human readable form after processing user get the required or desired data or set of information.

Central Processing Unit (CPU): The Central Processing unit is also called as brain or heart of a computer. The CPU is nothing but an electronic hardware device which carries or performs out all the operation such as arithmetic and logic operation. Below we have discussed briefly on arithmetic and logical operation. The CPU in another term is also called as "PROCESSOR". Every instruction given through the input devices such as keyboard or mouse is carried further for processing and we user get our desired results through are output devices such as printers and monitors. The CPU is also responsible for controlling all the operations of the other units of the computer system. When we talk or discuss CPU we tend to speak about its speed as speed these days matters most due to high number of large software which requires fast processor for execution.

The different component of CPU are Memory, Control Unit and Arithmetic logical unit.

Control Unit: The control Unit or CU Controls or coordinates all activities performed in a computer system. It receives information or instruction or directions from the main memory of computer. It tells the logic unit, memory as well as the input and output devices how to handle the program or instruction in proper order. When the control unit receives any set of information or instruction it converts them to control signals then this signal is sent to the central processor for further processing and finally, it understands which operation to execute, exactly or precisely and in which order.

Memory: The information or set of guidelines can be stored in PC storage unit when information or direction is exhibited to the PC system utilizing Input devices. To begin the procedure on information, Instructions given by input devices the information must be put away in memory, and later when the preparing is done the outcome produced is likewise put away in computer system for additionally handling. This type of work and action is done by storage unit. In another word, we can also describe the storage unit as the unit which gives space to store data or instruction of processed data, processed result.

a. It stores information or instruction
b. It stores Results
c. It stores consequence of prepared data

Arithmetic and Logic Unit (ALU): There are some processors now that has more than single AU [Arithmetic Unit]. ALU performs arithmetic and logical operation. When a set of instruction or program is conveyed out. Control unit generally characterized which sort of operation to Execute. Arithmetic operation comprises of (Addition, subtraction, division, multiplication) and the logical unit carries out the operation such (AND, OR, Equal, less than, greater then), and later the control is changed to ALU and the result generated in ALU later stored or puts away in transitory memory.

Characteristics of a Computer

Basic characteristics of computer are:

1. **Speed:** Computer has very high processing speed. A computer can process more than 100 million instructions

in one second. No human being can compete to solving the complex computation, faster than computer. Its speed is usually measured in microseconds, nanoseconds and picoseconds.

2. **Automatic:** When a user gives a job to computer it can work on it without human interventions.

3. **Accuracy:** Processing done by the computer is quite accurate. As we know Computer is programmed, so whatever input we give to a computer, it gives us an accurate result. The Errors can occur due to improper or wrong or inaccurate input given to the computer, computer system primarily depends upon the inputs.

4. **Storage Capacity:** Memory one of the most essential characteristics of computer, in today's era computer can store any volume of data due to its high storage capabilities. Once the data saved to the computer memory it remains in the memory, until and unless someone deletes, users can retrieve the data anytime, at any location they require, As the human being tends to forget small information given to them, but computer stores all the information permanently.

5. **Diligence:** Computer can work for hours without tiredness with same speed and accuracy. As the computer is a machine its does not refuse to work and works for hours and hours with the same speed, concentration and accuracy. But on the other hand, human being can get easily tired of same work repeatedly can lose their concentration, speed, and accuracy because human suffer from tiredness, laziness, unlike machines.

6. **Versatility:** Computer can perform several tasks at the same time, such as user can work on documents, search for any documents in the hard disk, play songs, download software, surfing net, calculate, a computer can perform several functions at the same time with same speed, accuracy and with consistency.

7. **NO IQ:** The computer can perform tasks only on receiving input data and commands or instructions from the user, it does not have intelligence of its own.

8. **NO Feelings**: Computer does not have emotions, knowledge, experience. They do not feel anything unlike humans i.e., tiredness, boredom, laziness or jealousy.

Evolution of computer:

One of the earliest machines designed to assist people in calculations was the abacus which is still being used some 5000 years after its invention. In 1642 Blaise Pascal (a famous French mathematician) invented an adding machine based on mechanical gears in which numbers were represented by the cogs on the wheels.

Englishman, Charles Babbage, invented in the 1830's a "Difference Engine" made out of brass and pewter rods and gears, and also designed a further device which he called an "Analytical Engine". His design contained the five key characteristics of modern computers: -

- ✓ An input device
- ✓ Storage for numbers waiting to be processed
- ✓ A processor or number calculator
- ✓ A unit to control the task and the sequence of its calculations
- ✓ An output device

Augusta Ada Byron (later Countess of Lovelace) was an associate of Babbage who has become known as the first computer programmer. An American, Herman Hollerith, developed (around 1890) the first electrically driven device. It utilized punched cards and metal rods which passed through the holes to close an electrical circuit and thus cause a counter to advance. This machine was able to complete the calculation of the 1890 U.S. census in 6 weeks compared with 7 1/2 years for the 1880 census which was manually counted. In 1936 Howard Aiken of Harvard University convinced Thomas Watson of IBM to invest $1 million in the development of an electromechanical version of Babbage's analytical engine. The Harvard Mark 1 was completed in 1944 and was 8 feet high and 55 feet long. At about the same time (the late 1930's) John Atanasoff of Iowa State University and his assistant Clifford Berry built the first digital computer that worked electronically, the ABC (Atanasoff-Berry Computer). This machine was basically a small calculator

Generations of Computer:

The first electronic computer was designed and built at the University of Pennsylvania based on vacuum tube technology. Vacuum tubes were used to perform logic operations and to store data. Generations of computers has been divided into five according to the development of technologies used to fabricate the processors, memories and I/O units.

First Generation: 1945 – 55

Second Generation: 1955 – 65

Third Generation: 1965 – 75

Fourth Generation: 1975 – 89

Fifth Generation: 1989 to present

First Generation computers:

ENIAC - Electronic Numerical Integrator And Calculator

EDSAC – Electronic Delay Storage Automatic Calculator

EDVAC – Electronic Discrete Variable Automatic Computer

UNIVAC – Universal Automatic Computer IBM 701

1. Vacuum tubes were used – basic arithmetic operations took few milliseconds.
2. Bulky.
3. Consume more power with limited performance.
4. High cost.
5. Uses assembly language – to prepare programs. These were translated into machine level language for execution.
6. Mercury delay line memories and Electrostatic memories were used.
7. Fixed point arithmetic was used.

8. 100 to 1000-fold increase in speed relative to the earlier mechanical and relay based electromechanical technology.
9. Punched cards and paper tape were invented to feed programs and data and to get results.
10. Magnetic tape / magnetic drum was used as secondary memory.
11. Mainly used for scientific computations.

Second Generation

IBM 7094 series

IBM 1400 series

CDC 164

1. Transistors were used in place of vacuum tubes. (Invented at AT&T Bell lab in 1947)
2. Small in size
3. Lesser power consumption and better performance
4. Lower cost

5. Magnetic ferrite core memories were used as main memory which is a random-access nonvolatile memory

6. Magnetic tapes and magnetic disks were used as secondary memory

7. Hardware for floating point arithmetic operations was developed.

8. Index registers were introduced which increased flexibility of programming.

9. High level languages such as FORTRAN, COBOL etc were used - Compilers were developed to translate the high-level program into corresponding assembly language program which was then translated into machine language.

10. Separate input-output processors were developed that could operate in parallel with CPU.

11. Punched cards continued during this period also.

12. 1000-fold increase in speed.

13. Increasingly used in business, industry and commercial organizations for preparation of payroll, inventory control, marketing, production planning, research, scientific & engineering analysis and design etc.

Third Generation

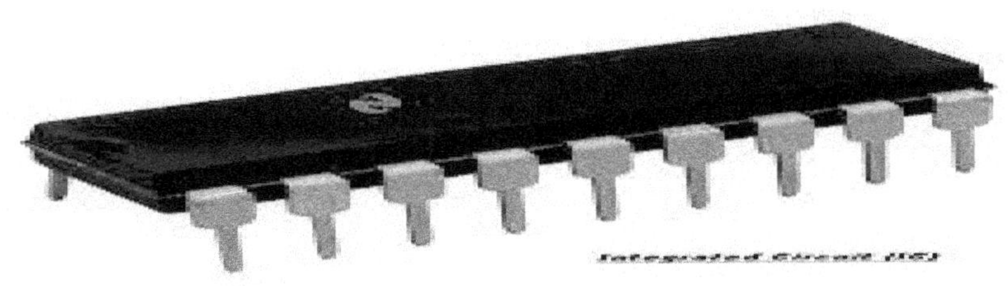

IBM 360 series

IBM 370 series

1. ICs were used
2. Small Scale Integration and Medium Scale Integration technology were implemented in CPU, I/O processors etc.
3. Smaller & better performance
4. Comparatively lesser cost
5. Faster processors
6. In the beginning magnetic core memories were used. Later they were replaced by semiconductor memories (RAM & ROM)
7. Introduced microprogramming
8. Microprogramming, parallel processing (pipelining, multiprocessor system etc.), multiprogramming, multi-user system (time shared system) etc. were introduced.
9. Operating system software were introduced (efficient sharing of a computer system by several user programs)
10. Cache and virtual memories were introduced (Cache memory makes the main memory appear faster than it really is. Virtual memory makes it appear larger)
11. High level languages were standardized by ANSI e.g., ANSI FORTRAN, ANSI COBOL etc.
12. Database management, multi-user application, online systems like closed loop process control, airline reservation, interactive query systems, automatic industrial control etc. emerged during this period.
13.

Fourth Generation

Intel's 8088,80286,80386,80486…

Motorola's 68000, 68030, 68040

Apple Macintosh

IBM PC

1. Microprocessors were introduced as CPU– Complete processors and large section of main memory could be implemented in a single chip
2. Tens of thousands of transistors can be placed in a single chip (VLSI design implemented)
3. CRT screen, laser & ink jet printers, scanners etc. were developed.
4. Semiconductor memory chips were used as the main memory
5. Secondary memory was composed of hard disks – Floppy disks & magnetic tapes were used for backup memory

6. Parallelism, pipelining cache memory and virtual memory were applied in a better way
7. LAN and WANS were developed (where desktop work stations interconnected)
8. Introduced C language and Unix OS
9. Introduced Graphical User Interface
10. Less power consumption
11. High performance, lower cost and very compact
12. Much increase in the speed of operation

Fifth Generation

IBM notebooks

Pentium PCs-Pentium 1/2/3/4/Dual core/Quad core

SUN work stations

Origin 2000

PARAM 10000

IBM SP/2

1. Generation number beyond IV, have been used occasionally to describe some current computer system that have a dominant organizational or application driven feature.
2. Computers based on artificial intelligence are available
3. Computers use extensive parallel processing, multiple pipelines, multiple processors etc.
4. Massive parallel machines and extensively distributed system connected by communication networks fall in this category.

5. Introduced ULSI (Ultra Large-Scale Integration) technology – Intel's Pentium 4 microprocessor contains 55 million transistors millions of components on a single IC chip.
6. Superscalar processors, Vector processors, SIMD processors, 32-bit micro controllers and embedded processors, Digital Signal Processors (DSP) etc. have been developed.
7. Memory chips up to 1 GB, hard disk drives up to 180 GB and optical disks up to 27 GB are available (still the capacity is increasing)
8. Object oriented language like JAVA suitable for internet programming has been developed.
9. Portable note book computers introduced
10. Storage technology advanced – large main memory and disk storage available
11. Introduced World Wide Web. (And other existing applications like e-mail, e Commerce, Virtual libraries/Classrooms, multimedia applications etc.)
12. New operating systems developed – Windows 95/98/XP/…, LINUX, etc.
13. Got hot pluggable features – which enable a failed component to be replaced with a new one without the need to shut down the system, allowing the uptime of the system to be very high.
14. The recent development in the application of internet is the Grid technology which is still in its upcoming stage.
15. Quantum mechanism and nanotechnology will radically change the phase of computers.

Classification of Computers:

The computer systems can be classified on the following basis:

1. On the basis of size.

2. On the basis of functionality.

3. On the basis of data handling.

Classification on the basis of size: -

Super computers: The super computers are the highest performing system. A supercomputer is a computer with a high level of performance compared to a general-purpose computer. The actual Performance of a supercomputer is measured in FLOPS instead of MIPS. All of the world's fastest 500 supercomputers run Linux-based operating systems. Additional research is being conducted in China, the US, the EU, Taiwan and Japan to build even faster, more high performing and more technologically superior supercomputers. Supercomputers actually play an important role in the field of computation, and are used for intensive computation tasks in various fields, including quantum mechanics, weather forecasting, climate research, oil and gas exploration, molecular modeling, and physical simulations. and also, Throughout the history, supercomputers have been essential in the field of the cryptanalysis. e.g.: PARAM, jaguar, roadrunner.

Mainframe computers : These are commonly called as big iron, they are usually used by big organizations for bulk data processing such as statics, census data processing, transaction processing and are widely used as the severs as these systems has a higher processing capability as compared to the other classes of computers, most of these mainframe architectures were established in 1960s, the research and development worked continuously over the years and the mainframes of today are far more better than the earlier ones, in size, capacity and efficiency. e.g.: IBM z Series, System z9 and System z10 servers.

Mini computers: These computers came into the market in mid 1960s and were sold at a much cheaper price than the main frames, they were actually designed for control, instrumentation, human interaction, and communication switching as distinct from calculation and record keeping, later they became very popular for personal uses with evolution.

In the 60s to describe the smaller computers that became possible with the use of transistors and core memory technologies, minimal instructions sets and less expensive peripherals such as the ubiquitous Teletype Model 33 ASR. They usually took up one or a few inch rack cabinets, compared with the large mainframes that could fill a room, there was a new term "MINICOMPUTERS" coined. e.g.: Personal Laptop, PC etc.

Micro-computers: A microcomputer is a small, relatively inexpensive computer with a microprocessor as its CPU. It includes a microprocessor, memory, and minimal I/O circuitry mounted on a single printed circuit board. The previous to these computers, mainframes and minicomputers, were comparatively much larger, hard to maintain and more expensive. They actually formed the foundation for present day microcomputers and smart gadgets that we use in day-to-day life. e.g.: Tablets, Smartwatches.

Classification on the basis of functionality: -

Servers: Servers are nothing but dedicated computers which are set-up to offer some services to the clients. They are named depending on the type of service they offered. e.g.: security server, database server.

Workstation: Those are the computers designed to primarily to be used by single user at a time. They run multi-user operating systems. They are the ones which we use for our day to day personal / commercial work.

Information Appliances: They are the portable devices which are designed to perform a limited set of tasks like basic calculations, playing multimedia, browsing internet etc. They are generally referred as the mobile devices. They have very limited memory and flexibility and generally run on "as-is" basis.

Embedded computers: They are the computing devices which are used in other machines to serve limited set of requirements. They follow instructions from the non-volatile memory and they are not required to execute reboot or reset. The processing units used in such device work to those basic requirements only and are different from the ones that are used in personal computers-better known as workstations.

Classification on the basis of data handling: -

Analog: An analog computer is a form of computer that uses the continuously-changeable aspects of physical fact such as electrical, mechanical, or hydraulic quantities to model the problem being solved. Anything that is variable with respect to time and continuous can be claimed as analog just like an analog clock measures time by means of the distance traveled for the spokes of the clock around the circular dial.

Digital: A computer that performs calculations and logical operations with quantities represented as digits, usually in the binary number system of "0" and "1", "Computer capable of solving problems by processing information expressed in discrete form. from manipulation of the combinations of the binary digits, it can perform mathematical calculations, organize and analyze data, control industrial and other processes, and simulate dynamic systems such as global weather patterns.

Hybrid: A computer that processes both analog and digital data, Hybrid computer is a digital computer that accepts analog signals, converts them to digital and processes them in digital form.

Applications of Computer:
The various applications of computers in today's arena:

1. **Business:** A computer has high speed of calculation, diligence, accuracy, reliability, or versatility which made it an integrated part in all business organizations. Computer is used in business organizations for:
   i. Payroll calculations
   ii. Budgeting
   iii. Sales analysis
   iv. Financial forecasting
   v. Managing employee's database
   vi. Maintenance of stocks etc.

2. **Banking:** Today banking is almost totally dependent on computer. Banks provide following facilities:
   i. Banks provide online accounting facility, which includes current balances, deposits, overdrafts, interest charges, shares, and trustee records.

ii.   ATM machines are making it even easier for customers to deal with banks.

3. **Insurance:** Insurance companies are keeping all records up-to-date with the help of computers. The insurance companies, finance houses and stock broking firms are widely using computers for their concerns. Insurance companies are maintaining a database of all clients with information showing.

i.   Procedure to continue with policies
ii.   Starting date of the policies
iii.   Next due installment of a policy
iv.   Maturity date
v.   Interests due
vi.   Survival benefits
vii.   Bonus

4. **Education:** The computer has provided a lot of facilities in the education system.

i.   The computer provides a tool in the education system known as CBE Computer-Based Education.
ii.   CBE involves control, delivery, and evaluation of learning.
iii.   The computer education is rapidly increasing the graph of number of computer students.
iv.   There are number of methods in which educational institutions can use computer to educate the students.
v.   It is used to prepare a database about performance of a student and analysis is carried out on this basis.

5. **Marketing:** In marketing, uses of computer are following:

i. Advertising - With computers, advertising professionals create art and graphics, write and revise copy, and print and disseminate ads with the goal of selling more products.

ii. At Home Shopping - Home shopping has been made possible through use of computerized catalogues that provide access to product information and permit direct entry of orders to be filled by the customers.

6. **Health Care:** Computers have become important part in hospitals, labs, and dispensaries. The computers are being used in hospitals to keep the record of patients and medicines. It is also used in scanning and diagnosing different diseases. ECG, EEG, Ultrasounds and CT scans etc., are also done by computerized machines. Some major fields of health care in which computers are used are:

i. Diagnostic System - Computers are used to collect data and identify cause of illness.

ii. Lab-diagnostic System - All tests can be done and reports are prepared by computer.

iii. Patient Monitoring System - These are used to check patient's signs for abnormality such as in Cardiac Arrest, ECG etc.

iv. Pharma Information System - Computer checks Drug-Labels, Expiry dates, harmful drug's side effects etc.

v. Surgery: Nowadays, computers are also used in performing surgery.

7. **Engineering Design:** Computers are widely used in Engineering purpose. One of major areas is CAD Computer-aided design. That provides creation and modification of images. Some fields are:

i. Structural Engineering - Requires stress and strain analysis for design of Ships, Buildings, Budgets, Airplanes etc.

ii. Industrial Engineering - Computers deal with design, implementation and improvement of integrated systems of people, materials and equipment's.

iii. Architectural Engineering - Computers help in planning towns, designing buildings, determining a range of buildings on a site using both 2D and 3D drawings.

8. **Military:** Computers are largely used in defense. Modern tanks, missiles, weapons etc. Military also employs computerized control systems. Some military areas where a computer has been used are:

i. Missile Control

ii. Military Communication

iii. Military Operation and Planning

iv. Smart Weapons

9. **Communication:** Communication means to convey a message, an idea, a picture or speech that is received and understood clearly and correctly by the person for whom it is meant for. Some main areas in this category are:

i. E-mail

ii. Chatting

iii. Usenet

iv. FTP

v. Telnet

vi. Video-conferencing

10. **Government:** Computers play an important role in government. Some major fields in this category are:

i. Budgets

ii. Sales tax department

iii. Income tax department

iv. Male/Female ratio

v. Computerization of voter's lists

vi. Computerization of driving licensing system

vii. Computerization of PAN card

viii. Weather forecasting

BIOS

BIOS (basic input/output system) is the program a computer's microprocessor uses to start the computer system after it is powered on. It also manages data flow between the computer's operating system (OS) and attached devices, such as the hard disk, video adapter, keyboard, mouse and printer.

History of BIOS

The term BIOS was first coined in 1975 by American computer scientist Gary Kildall. It was incorporated into IBM's first personal computer in 1981 and, in the years to come, gained popularity within other PCs, becoming an integral part of computers for some time. However, BIOS' popularity has waned in favor of a newer technology: Unified Extensible Firmware Interface (UEFI). Intel announced a plan in 2017 to retire support for legacy BIOS systems by 2020, replacing them with UEFI.

Uses of BIOS

The main use of BIOS is to act as a middleman between OSes and the hardware they run on. BIOS is theoretically always the intermediary between the microprocessor and I/O device control information and data flow. Although, in some cases, BIOS can arrange for data to flow directly to memory from devices, such as video cards, that require faster data flow to be effective.

Working BIOS

BIOS comes included with computers, as firmware on a chip on the motherboard. In contrast, an OS like Windows or iOS can either be pre-installed by the manufacturer or vendor or installed by the user. BIOS is a program that is made accessible to the microprocessor on an erasable programmable read-only memory (EPROM) chip. When users turn on their computer, the microprocessor passes control to the BIOS program, which is always located at the same place on EPROM.

When BIOS boots up a computer, it first determines whether all of the necessary attachments are in place and operational. Any piece of hardware containing files the computer needs to start is called a boot device. After testing and ensuring boot devices are functioning, BIOS loads the OS -- or key parts of it -- into the computer's random-access memory (RAM) from a hard disk or diskette drive (the boot device).

Functions of BIOS

BIOS identifies, configures, tests and connects computer hardware to the OS immediately after a computer is turned on. The combination of these steps is called the boot process.

These tasks are each carried out by BIOS' four main functions:

1.	Power-on self-test (POST). This tests the hardware of the computer before loading the OS.

2.	Bootstrap loader. This locates the OS.

3.	Software/drivers. This locates the software and drivers that interface with the OS once running.

4.	Complementary metal-oxide semiconductor (CMOS) setup. This is a configuration program that enable users to alter hardware and system settings. CMOS is the name of BIOS' non-volatile memory.

Chapter 2: Input Output Devices and Memory

Input Devices:

Following are some of the important input devices which are used in a computer:

1. **Keyboard:** Keyboard is the most common and very popular input device which helps to input data to the computer. The layout of the keyboard is like that of traditional typewriter, although there are some additional keys provided for performing additional functions. Keyboards are of two sizes 84 keys or 101/102 keys, but now keyboards with 104 keys or 108 keys are also available for Windows and Internet.

The keys on the keyboard are in table below

S.No	Keys & Description
1.	Typing Keys: These keys include the letter keys A–Z and digit keys 09 which generally give the same layout as that of typewriters.
2.	Numeric Keypad: It is used to enter the numeric data or cursor movement. Generally, it consists of a set of 17 keys that are laid out in the same configuration used by most adding machines and calculators.
3.	Function Keys: The twelve function keys are present on the keyboard which are arranged in a row at the top of the keyboard. Each function key has a unique meaning and is used for some specific purpose.
4.	Control keys: These keys provide cursor and screen control. It includes four directional arrow keys. Control keys also include Home, End, Insert, Delete, Page Up, Page Down, ControlCtrl, AlternateAlt, EscapeEsc.
5.	Special Purpose Keys: Keyboard also contains some special purpose keys such as Enter, Shift, Caps Lock, Num Lock, Space bar, Tab, and Print Screen.

2. **Mouse:** Mouse is the most popular pointing device. It is a very famous cursor-control device having a small palm size box with a round ball at its base, which senses the movement of the mouse and sends corresponding signals to the CPU when the mouse buttons are pressed.

Generally, it has two buttons called the left and the right button and a wheel is present between the buttons. A mouse can be used to control the position of the cursor on the screen, but it cannot be used to enter text into the computer.

3. **Joystick:** Joystick is also a pointing device, which is used to move the cursor position on a monitor screen. It is a stick having a spherical ball at its both lower and upper ends. The lower spherical ball moves in a socket. The joystick can be moved in all four directions. The function of the joystick is similar to that of a mouse. It is mainly used in Computer Aided Designing CAD and playing computer games.

4. **Digitizer:** Digitizer is an input device which converts analog information into digital form. Digitizer can convert a signal from the television or camera into a series of numbers that could be stored in a computer. They can be used by the computer to create a picture of whatever the camera had been pointed at. Digitizer is also known as Tablet or Graphics Tablet as it converts graphics and pictorial data into binary inputs. A graphic tablet as digitizer is used for fine works of drawing and image manipulation applications.

5. **Light Pen:** Light pen is a pointing device similar to a pen. It is used to select a displayed menu item or draw pictures on the monitor screen. It consists of a photocell and an optical system placed in a small tube. When the tip of a light pen is moved over the monitor screen and the pen button is pressed, its photocell sensing element detects the screen location and sends the corresponding signal to the CPU.

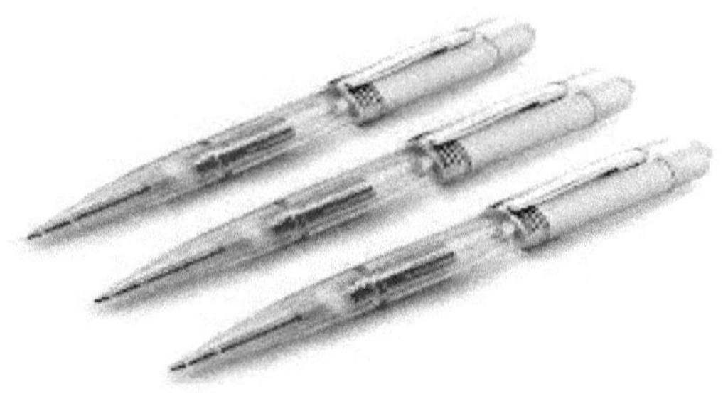

6. **Touch screen:** A touch screen is a computer display screen that is also an input device. The screens are sensitive to pressure; a user interacts with the computer by touching pictures or words on the screen.

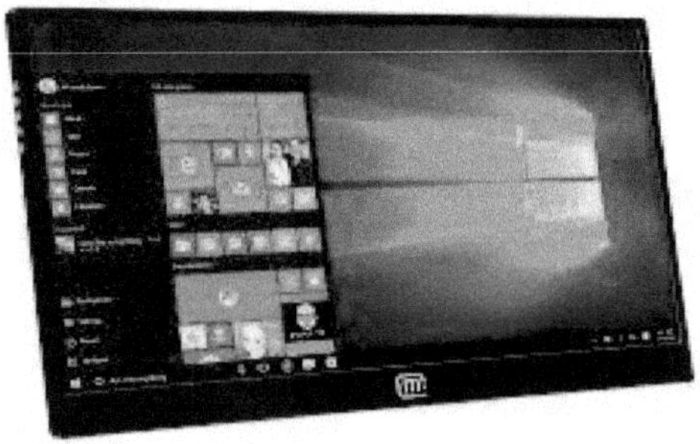

7. **Track Ball:** Track ball is an input device that is mostly used in notebook or laptop computer, instead of a mouse. This is a ball which is half inserted and by moving fingers on the ball, the pointer can be moved. Since the whole device is not moved, a track ball requires less space than a mouse. A track ball comes in various shapes like a ball, a button, or a square.

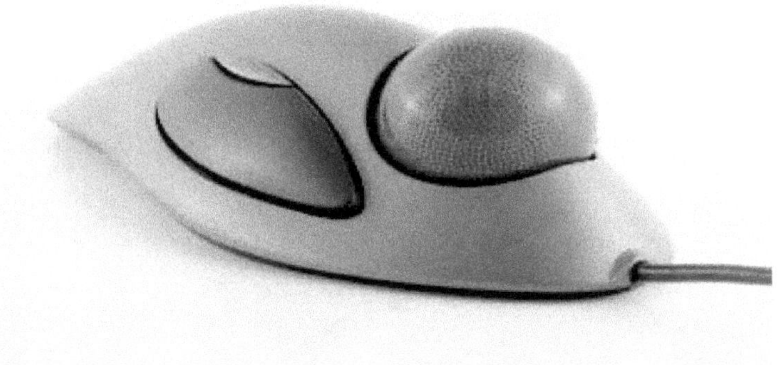

8. **Microphone:** Microphone is an input device to input sound that is then stored in a digital form. The microphone is used for various applications such as adding sound to a multimedia presentation or for mixing music.

9. **Scanner:** Scanner is an input device, which works more like a photocopy machine. It is used when some information is available on paper and it is to be transferred to the hard disk of the computer for further manipulation. Scanner captures images from the source which are then converted into a digital form that can be stored on the disk. These images can be edited before they are printed.

10. **Magnetic Ink Card Reader (MICR):** MICR input device is generally used in banks as there are large number of cheques to be processed every day. The bank's code number and cheque number are printed on the cheques with a special type of ink that contains particles of magnetic material that are machine readable. This reading process is called Magnetic Ink Character Recognition MICR. The main advantages of MICR is that it is fast and less error prone.

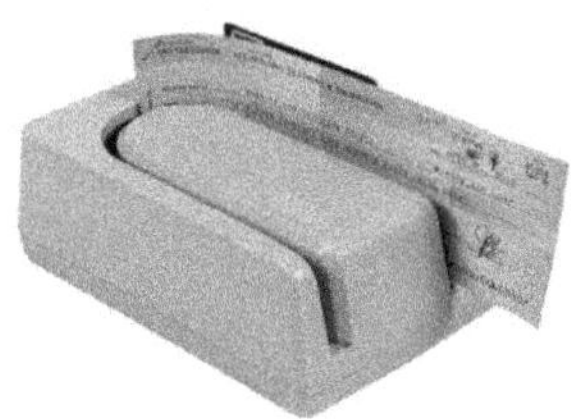

11. **Optical Character Reader (OCR):** OCR is an input device used to read a printed text OCR scans the text optically, character by character, converts them

into a machine-readable code, and stores the text on the system memory.

12. **Optical Mark Reader (OMR):** OMR is a special type of optical scanner used to recognize the type of mark made by pen or pencil. It is used where one out of a few alternatives is to be selected and marked. It is specially used for checking the answer sheets of examinations having multiple choice questions.

13. **Bar Code Readers:** Bar Code Reader is a device used for reading bar coded data. Bar coded data is generally used

in labelling goods, numbering the books, etc. It may be a handheld scanner or may be embedded in a stationary scanner. Bar Code Reader scans a bar code image, converts it into an alphanumeric value, which is then fed to the computer that the bar code reader is connected to.

14. **Webcam:** A webcam is an input device because it captures a video image of the scene in front of it. It is either built in to the computer (e.g., laptop) or it is connected through an USB cable. The video signal is made up of a series of individual 'image frames' which are an instant snapshot of the scene in front of it. Each image frame is sent to the computer for further processing by webcam software. If the 'frame rate' is fast enough (more than 25 frames per second) it appears as motion video.

15. **Digital camera:** A digital camera is most commonly used as an input device as it takes in information through its lens and then records it on its storage device. Sometimes, though, a digital camera is also an output device. This occurs when people connect a digital camera to a computer to transfer pictures to the computer.

16. **Touchpad:** A touchpad (also called a trackpad) is a type of input device for computers that does the same things as a computer mouse. It is made up of a flat, touch-sensitive surface which the user slides one or more

fingers on to move the cursor on the screen. Next to the touchpad are push-buttons that work just like mouse buttons, including left-clicking and right-clicking. In some newer touchpads, there are no actual buttons, and clicking is done by pushing near the button of the touchpad itself.

17. **Smart card:** Smart cards are often called input devices. In fact, they are actually simple storage devices. A smart card looks like a magnetic stripe card but it contains a small RAM chip. When the card is put into a machine data can be read from the card or written onto it. A smart card can store much more data than a magnetic stripe card can. The most popular card in use at the moment can store up to 4Kb (about 4000 characters) of information but cards with capacities up to 1Mb (1,000,000 characters) are available. Petrol companies and supermarkets use smart cards to store information about points that customers earn when they buy goods. Every time the customer buys something the number of points stored on the card is increased. The customer can then spend these points to buy goods. Many banks now

issue debit cards that are smart cards as these are more secure than traditional magnetic stripe cards.

Output Devices:

Following are some of the important output devices used in a computer.

1. Visual Display Unit (VDU)
2. Printers
3. Plotters
1. **Visual Display Unit (VDU):** VDU are the main output device of a computer. It forms images from tiny dots, called pixels that are arranged in a rectangular form. The sharpness of the image depends upon the number of pixels.

There are two kinds of viewing screen used for monitors.

    i.   Cathode-Ray Tube CRT
  ii.   Flat-Panel Display
    i.   **Cathode-Ray Tube (CRT):** The CRT display is made up of small picture elements called pixels. The smaller the pixels, the better the image clarity or resolution. It takes more than one illuminated

pixel to form a whole character, such as the letter 'e' in the word help. A finite number of characters can be displayed on a screen at once. The screen can be divided into a series of character boxes - fixed location on the screen where a standard character can be placed. Most screens are capable of displaying 80 characters of data horizontally and 25 lines vertically.

There are some disadvantages of CRT –

    a. Large in Size

    b. High power consumption.

2. **Flat-Panel Display:** The flat-panel display refers to a class of video devices that have reduced volume, weight and power requirement in comparison to the CRT. You can hang them on walls or wear them on your wrists. Current uses of flat-panel displays include calculators, video games, monitors, laptop computer, and graphics display. The flat-panel display is divided into two categories –

a. Emissive Displays – Emissive displays are devices that convert electrical energy into light. For example, plasma panel and LED (Light–Emitting Diodes).

b. Non-Emissive Displays – Non-emissive displays use optical effects to convert sunlight or light from some other source into graphics patterns. For example, LCD (Liquid–Crystal Device).

2. **Printer:** Printer is an output device, which is used to print information on paper. Some of the printers are explained below:

i. **Dot matrix printer:** In the market, one of the most popular printers is Dot Matrix Printer. These printers are popular because of their ease of printing and economical price. Each character printed is in the form of pattern of dots and head consists of a Matrix of Pins of size (5*7, 7*9, 9*7 or 9*9) which come out to form a character which is why it is called Dot Matrix Printer.

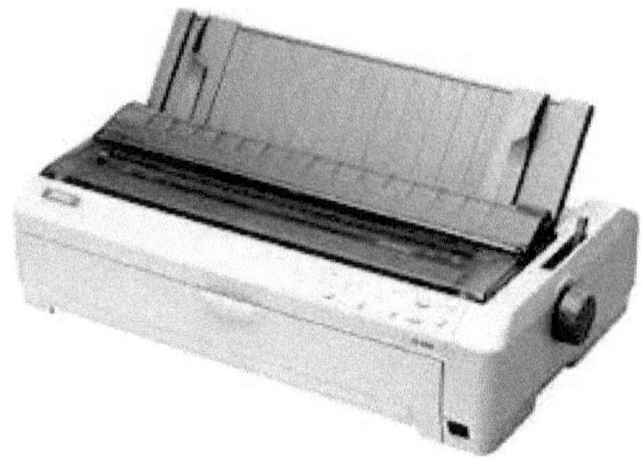

ii.   **Laser printers:** A laser printer is a type of printer that uses a laser and electrical charge model instead of the traditional printing of ink onto paper. Laser printers have increased the neatness and sophistication of print projects, with typical resolutions of 600 dots per inch or higher.

iii.   **Inkjet printer:** They print characters by spraying small drops of ink onto paper. Inkjet printers produce high quality output with presentable features. They make less noise because no hammering is done and these have many styles of printing modes available. Color printing is also possible. Some models of Inkjet printers can produce multiple copies of printing also.

3. **Plotter:** A plotter is a computer hardware device much like a printer that is used for printing vector graphics. Instead of toner, plotters use a pen, pencil, marker, or another writing tool to draw multiple, continuous lines onto paper rather than a series of dots like a traditional printer. Though once widely used for computer-aided design, these devices have more or less been phased out by wide-format printers. Plotters are used to produce a hard copy of schematics and other similar applications.

Memory:

Memory is primarily of three types –

1. Cache Memory
2. Primary Memory/Main Memory
3. Secondary Memory

1. **Cache Memory:** Cache memory is a very high-speed semiconductor memory which can speed up the CPU. It acts as a buffer between the CPU and the main memory. It is used to hold those parts of data and program which are most frequently used by the CPU. The parts of data and programs are transferred from the disk to cache memory by the operating system, from where the CPU can access them.

2. **Primary Memory:** Primary memory holds only those data and instructions on which the computer is currently working. It has a limited capacity and data is lost when power is switched off. It is generally made up of semiconductor device. These memories are not as fast as registers. The data and instruction required to be processed resides in the main memory. It is divided into two subcategories RAM and ROM.

i.   **RAM (Random Access Memory):** RAM is the internal memory of the CPU for storing data, program, and program result. It is a read/write memory which stores data until the machine is working. As soon as the machine is switched off, data is erased. Access time in RAM is independent of the address, that is, each storage location inside the memory is as easy to reach as other locations and takes the same amount of time. Data in the RAM can be accessed randomly but it is very expensive. RAM is volatile, i.e. data stored in it is lost when we switch off the computer or if there is a power failure. Hence, a backup Uninterruptible Power System (UPS) is often used with computers. RAM is small, both in terms of its physical size and in the amount of data it can hold. RAM is of two types –
a) Static RAM (SRAM)
b) Dynamic RAM (DRAM)

Static RAM (SRAM): The word static indicates that the memory retains its contents as long as power is being supplied. However, data is lost when the power gets down due to volatile nature. SRAM chips use a matrix of 6-transistors and no capacitors. Transistors do not require power to prevent leakage, so SRAM need not be refreshed on a regular basis. There is extra space in the matrix, hence SRAM uses more chips than DRAM for the same amount of storage space, making the manufacturing costs higher. SRAM is thus used as cache memory and has very fast access.

Dynamic RAM (DRAM): DRAM, unlike SRAM, must be continually refreshed in order to maintain the data.

This is done by placing the memory on a refresh circuit that rewrites the data several hundred times per second. DRAM is used for most system memory as it is cheap and small. All DRAMs are made up of memory cells, which are composed of one capacitor and one transistor.

ii. **ROM:** ROM stands for Read Only Memory. The memory from which we can only read but cannot write on it. This type of memory is non-volatile. The information is stored permanently in such memories during manufacture. A ROM stores such instructions that are required to start a computer. This operation is referred to as bootstrap. ROM chips are not only used in the computer but also in other electronic items like washing machine and microwave oven. Let us now discuss the various types of ROMs.

a. **MROM (Masked ROM):** The very first ROMs were hard-wired devices that contained a pre-programmed set of data or instructions. These kinds of ROMs are known as masked ROMs, which are inexpensive.

b. **PROM (Programmable Read Only Memory):** PROM is read-only memory that can be modified only once by a user. The user buys a blank PROM and enters the desired contents using a PROM program. Inside the PROM chip, there are small fuses which are burnt open during programming. It can be programmed only once and is not erasable.

c. **EPROM (Erasable and Programmable Read Only Memory):** EPROM can be erased by exposing it to ultra-violet light for a duration of up to 40 minutes. Usually, an EPROM eraser achieves this function.

During programming, an electrical charge is trapped in an insulated gate region. The charge is retained for more than 10 years because the charge has no leakage path. For erasing this charge, ultra-violet light is passed through a quartz crystal window (lid). This exposure to ultra-violet light dissipates the charge. During normal use, the quartz lid is sealed with a sticker.

d. **EEPROM (Electrically Erasable and Programmable Read Only Memory):** EEPROM is programmed and erased electrically. It can be erased and reprogrammed about ten thousand times. Both erasing and programming take about 4 to 10 ms (millisecond). In EEPROM, any location can be selectively erased and programmed. EEPROMs can be erased one byte at a time, rather than erasing the entire chip. Hence, the process of reprogramming is flexible but slow.

3. Secondary Memory:

This type of memory is also known as external memory or non-volatile. It is slower than the main memory. These are used for storing data/information permanently. CPU directly does not access these memories, instead they are accessed via input-output routines. The contents of secondary memories are first transferred to the main memory, and then the CPU can access it. Let us discuss now various types of secondary memories:

a. **Hard Disk Drive:** Hard disk drive is made up of a series of circular disks called platters arranged one over the other almost ½ inches apart around a spindle. Disks are made of non-magnetic material like aluminum alloy and coated with 10-20 nm of magnetic material. Standard diameter of these disks is 14 inches and they rotate with speeds varying from 4200 rpm (rotations per minute) for personal computers to 15000 rpm for servers. Data is stored by magnetizing or demagnetizing the magnetic coating. A magnetic reader arm is used to read data from and write data to the disks. A typical modern HDD has capacity in terabytes (TB).

b. **Optical disk:** An optical disk is any computer disk that uses optical storage techniques and technology to read and write data. It is a computer storage disk that stores data digitally and uses laser beams (transmitted from a laser head mounted on an optical disk drive) to read and write data.

c. **Blu Ray Disk:** Blu Ray Disk (BD) is an optical storage media used to store high definition (HD) video and other multimedia filed. BD uses shorter wavelength laser as compared to CD/DVD. This enables writing arm to focus more tightly on the disk and hence pack in more data. BDs can store up to 128 GB data.

d. **Pen Drive:** Pen drive is a portable memory device that uses solid state memory rather than magnetic fields or lasers to record data. It uses a technology similar to RAM, except that it is nonvolatile. It is also called USB drive, key drive or flash memory.

Memory card: A memory card is a type of storage device that is used for storing media and data files. It provides a permanent and non-volatile medium to store data and files from the attached device. Memory cards are commonly used in small,

portable devices, such as cameras and phones. A memory card
is also known as a flash card.

Chapter 3: Computer Software and Languages

Software:

Software is a set of instructions, data or programs used to operate computers and execute specific tasks. Software is a generic term used to refer to applications, scripts and programs that run on a device. Software enables the user to interact with a computer, its hardware, or perform tasks.

Relationship Between Hardware and Software

1. Hardware and software both are interdependent on each other. Each of them should work along to form computer produce a helpful output.
2. The software cannot be used if there is no support of any hardware device.
3. When there are no proper instructions given, the hardware cannot be used and is useless.
4. To get a selected job done on the pc, the relevant software package has to be loaded into the hardware.
5. The different software package can be loaded on hardware to run totally different jobs.
6. The software acts as an associate interface between the user and therefore the hardware.
7. We can say the hardware and software are the heart and soul of a digital computer.

Types of Software:

There are two main types of software: systems software and application software.

Systems Software:

Systems software includes the programs that are dedicated to managing the computer itself, such as the operating system, file management utilities, and disk operating system (or DOS). The operating system manages the computer hardware resources in addition to applications and data. Without systems software installed in our computers we would have to type the instructions for everything we wanted the computer to do. Some commonly used system software's are:

I. **Operating System:** An Operating System (OS) is an interface between a computer user and computer hardware. An operating system is a software which performs all the basic tasks like file management, memory management, process management, handling input and output, and controlling peripheral devices such as disk drives and printers. Some popular Operating Systems include Linux Operating System, Windows Operating System, VMS, OS/400, AIX, z/OS, etc.

Following are some of important functions of an operating System.

    a. Memory Management
    b. Processor Management

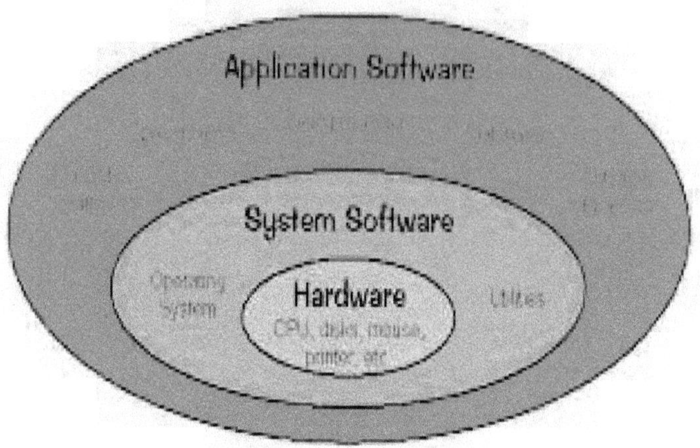

    c. Device Management

    d. File Management

    e. Security

    f. Control over system performance

    g. Job accounting

    h. Error detecting aids

    i. Coordination between other software and users.

a. **Memory Management**: Memory management refers to management of Primary Memory or Main Memory. Main memory is a large array of words or bytes where each word or byte has its own address. Main memory provides a fast storage that can be accessed directly by the CPU. For a program to be executed, it must in the main memory. An Operating System does the following activities for memory management:

    i. Keeps tracks of primary memory, i.e., what part of it are in use by whom, what part are not in use.

    ii. In multiprogramming, the OS decides which process will get memory when and how much.

iii. Allocates the memory when a process requests it to do so.

iv. De-allocates the memory when a process no longer needs it or has been terminated.

b. **Processor Management:** In multiprogramming environment, the OS decides which process gets the processor when and for how much time. This function is called process scheduling. An Operating System does the following activities for processor management:

i. Keeps tracks of processor and status of process. The program responsible for this task is known as traffic controller.

ii. Allocates the processor (CPU) to a process.

iii. De-allocates processor when a process is no longer required.

c. **Device Management:** An Operating System manages device communication via their respective drivers. It does the following activities for device management:

i. Keeps tracks of all devices. The program responsible for this task is known as the I/O controller.

ii. Decides which process gets the device when and for how much time.

iii. Allocates the device in the most efficient way.

iv. De-allocates devices.

d. **File Management:** A file system is normally organized into directories for easy navigation and usage. These directories may contain files and other directions. An Operating System does the following activities for file management:

     i.   Keeps track of information, location, uses, status etc. The collective facilities are often known as file system.

    ii.   Decides who gets the resources.

   iii.   Allocates the resources.

   iv.   De-allocates the resources.

e. **Security:** By means of password and similar other techniques, it prevents unauthorized access to programs and data.

f. **Control over system performance:** Recording delays between request for a service and response from the system.

g. **Job accounting:** Keeping track of time and resources used by various jobs and users.

h. **Error detecting aids:** Production of dumps, traces, error messages, and other debugging and error detecting aids.

i. **Coordination between other software and users:** Coordination and assignment of compilers, interpreters, assemblers and other software to the various users of the computer systems.

Types of Operating System: some of the important types of operating systems which are most commonly used.

1. **Batch processing:** Batch processing is a technique in which an Operating System collects the programs and data together in a batch before processing starts. An operating system does the following activities related to batch processing:

    a. The OS defines a job which has predefined sequence of commands, programs and data as a single unit.

b. The OS keeps a number a jobs in memory and executes them without any manual information.

c. Jobs are processed in the order of submission, i.e., first come first served fashion.

d. When a job completes its execution, its memory is released and the output for the job gets copied into an output spool for later printing or processing.

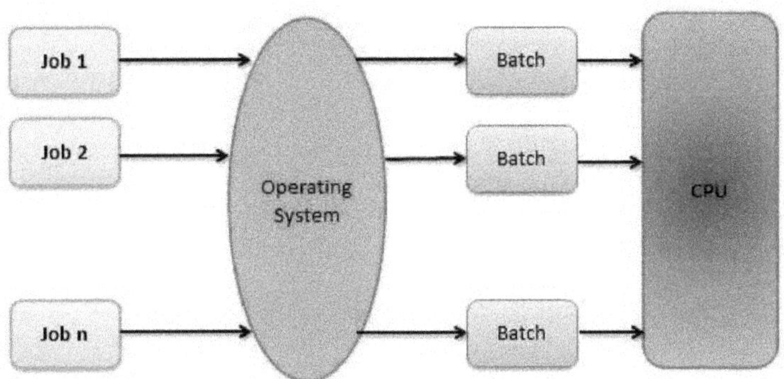

2. **Multiprogramming:** Sharing the processor, when two or more programs reside in memory at the same time, is referred as multiprogramming. Multiprogramming assumes a single shared processor. Multiprogramming increases CPU utilization by organizing jobs so that the CPU always has one to execute. An OS does the following activities related to multiprogramming.

a. The operating system keeps several jobs in memory at a time.

b. This set of jobs is a subset of the jobs kept in the job pool.

c. The operating system picks and begins to execute one of the jobs in the memory.

d. Multiprogramming operating systems monitor the state of all active programs and system resources using memory management programs to ensures that the CPU is never idle, unless there are no jobs to process.

The following figure shows the memory layout for a multiprogramming system.

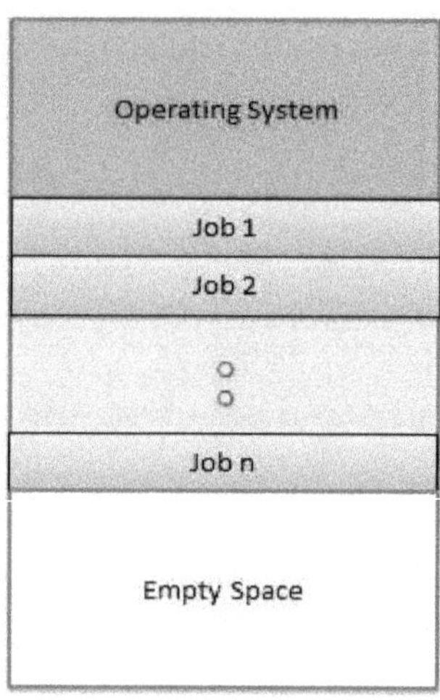

3. **Multiprocessor Operating System**: It refers to the use of two or more central processing units (CPU) within a single computer system. These multiple CPUs are in a close communication sharing the computer bus, memory and other peripheral devices. These systems are referred as tightly coupled systems. These types of systems are used when very high speed is required to process a large volume of data. These systems are generally used in environment like satellite control, weather forecasting

etc. The basic organization of multiprocessing system is shown in fig.

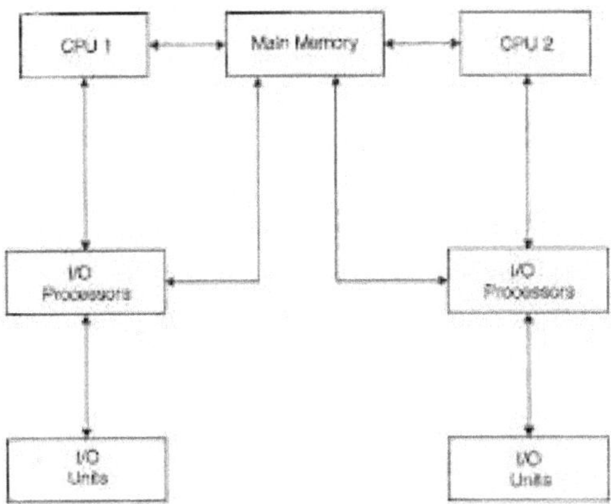

4. **Time Sharing:** A time sharing system allows many users to share the computer resources simultaneously. In other words, time sharing refers to the allocation of computer resources in time slots to several programs simultaneously. For example, a mainframe computer that has many users logged on to it. Each user uses the resources of the mainframe -i.e. memory, CPU etc. The users feel that they are exclusive user of the CPU, even though this is not possible with one CPU i.e. shared among different users. The time-sharing systems were developed to provide an interactive use of the computer system. A time-shared system uses CPU scheduling and multiprogramming to provide each user with a small portion of a time-shared computer. It allows many users to share the computer resources simultaneously. As the system switches rapidly from one user to the other, a short time slot is given to each user for their executions. The time-sharing system provides the direct access to a large number of users where CPU time is divided among

all the users on scheduled basis. The OS allocates a set of time to each user. When this time is expired, it passes control to the next user on the system. The time allowed is extremely small and the users are given the impression that they each have their own CPU and they are the sole owner of the CPU. This short period of time during that a user gets attention of the CPU is known as a time slice or a quantum. The concept of time-sharing system is shown in figure.

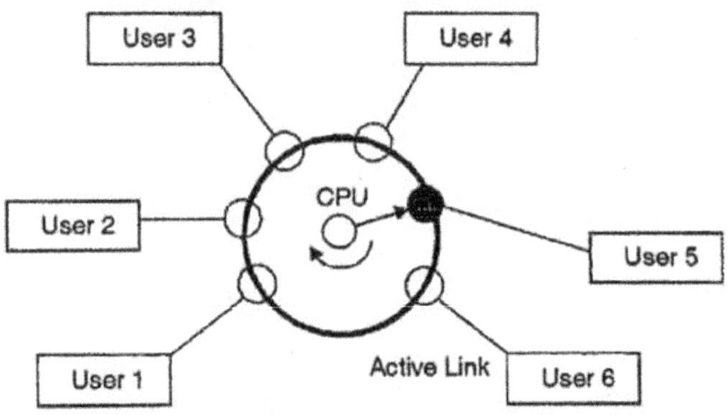

5. **Real Time operating System:** A real-time system is defined as a data processing system in which the time interval required to process and respond to inputs is so small that it controls the environment. The time taken by the system to respond to an input and display of required updated information is termed as the response time. So, in this method, the response time is very less as compared to online processing. Real-time systems are used when there are rigid time requirements on the operation of a processor or the flow of data and real-time systems can be used as a control device in a dedicated

application. A real-time operating system must have well-defined, fixed time constraints, otherwise the system will fail. For example, Scientific experiments, medical imaging systems, industrial control systems, weapon systems, robots, air traffic control systems, etc. There are two types of real-time operating systems.

a. **Hard real-time systems:** Hard real-time systems guarantee that critical tasks complete on time. In hard real-time systems, secondary storage is limited or missing and the data is stored in ROM. In these systems, virtual memory is almost never found.

b. **Soft real-time systems:** Soft real-time systems are less restrictive. A critical real-time task gets priority over other tasks and retains the priority until it completes. Soft real-time systems have limited utility than hard real-time systems. For example, multimedia, virtual reality, Advanced Scientific Projects like undersea exploration and planetary rovers, etc.

Single-User operating System: Single user operating' system allows a single user to access the computer at a time. This type of operating system is mostly used on computers having single processor such as PCs. In single user operating system, the CPU remains idle during an I/O operation. So, the CPU utilization is reduced.

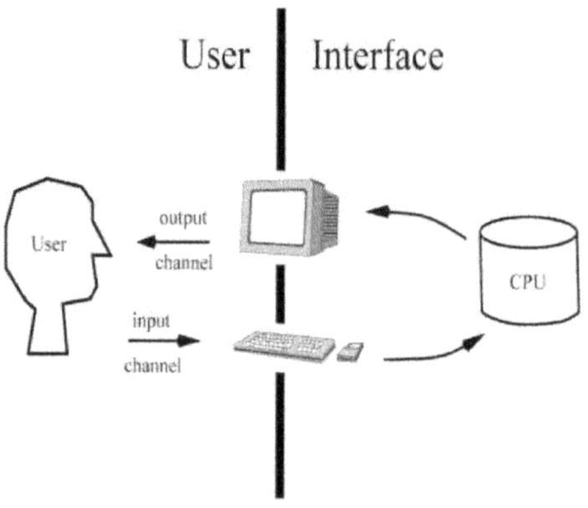

Single user operating system is further divided into two classes.

a. **Single-User Single Tasking Operating System:** The single-user single tasking operating system allows a single user to execute one program at a time. MS-DOS is an example of this kind of operating system.

b. **Single-User Multitasking Operating System:** In multitasking, more than one program can be executed at a time on a single computer. Single-user multitasking operating system allows a single user to execute multiple programs at the same time. The Windows and Mac-OS are examples of single-user multitasking operating systems. For example, in Windows you can load multiple programs at a time such as Ms-Excel, Ms-Word, Ms-Access as well as you can listen the music.

Multi-user operating system: A Multi-user operating system is a computer operating system which allows multiple users to access the single system with one operating system on it. It is generally used on large mainframe computers. Example: Linux, Unix, Windows 2000, Ubuntu, Mac OS etc., In the multi-user operating system, different users connected at different terminals and we can access, these users through the network as shown in the diagram.

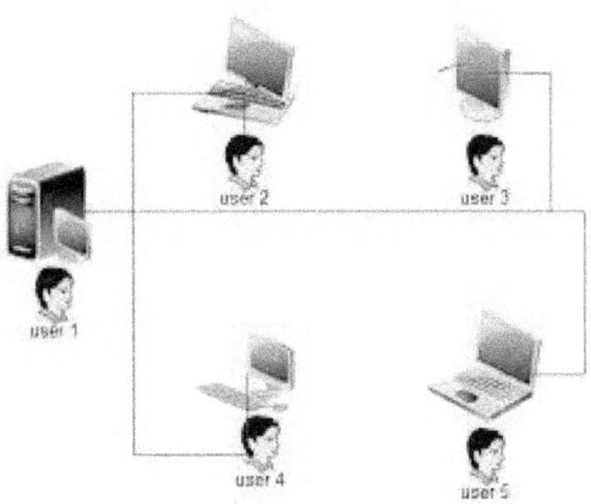

A multi-user operating system is of 3 types which are as follows:

1. **Distributed Systems**: in this, different computers are managed in such a way so that they can appear as a single computer. So, a sort of network is formed through which they can communicate with each other.

2. **Time-sliced Systems:** in this, a short period is assigned to each task, i.e. each user is given a time slice of the CPU time. As we know these time slices are tiny, so it appears to the users that they all are using the mainframe computer at the same time.

3. **Multiprocessor Systems:** in this, the operating system utilises more than one processor. Example: Linux, Unix, Windows XP

ii. **Language Translators:** These are intermediate programs relied on by software programmers to translate high-level language source code to machine language code. The former is a collection of programming languages that are easy for humans to comprehend and code (i.e., Java, C++, Python, PHP, BASIC). The latter is a complex code only understood by the processor.

Popular translator languages are compilers, assemblers, and interpreters. They're usually designed by computer manufacturers. Translator programs may perform a complete translation of program codes or translate every other instruction at a time.

Machine code is written in a number system of base-2, written out in 0 or 1. This is the lowest level language possible. While seemingly meaningless to humans, the zeros and ones are actually sequenced intelligently by the processor to refer to every conceivable human code and word. Besides simplifying the work of software developers, translators help in various design tasks as:

a. Identify syntax errors during translation, thus allowing changes to be made to the code.
b. Provide diagnostic reports whenever the code rules are not followed.
c. Allocate data storage for the program.
d. List both source code and program details.

Utility Programs: This software analyse and maintain a computer. These software's are focused on how Operating System works on that basis it performs task to enable smooth functioning of computer. These software's may come along with Operating System like windows defender, windows disk cleanup tool, Antivirus, backup software, file manager, disk compression tool all are utility software.

Communication software: It is an application or program designed to pass information from one system to another. Such software provides remote access to systems and transmits files in a multitude of formats between computers. Communication software forms a part of communication systems with software components classified according to functions within the Open Systems Interconnection Model (OSI Model). The best-defined examples of communication software are file transfer protocol (FTP), messaging software and email.

Application Software:

Application software products are designed to satisfy a particular need of a particular environment. All software applications prepared in the computer lab can come under the category of Application software. Application software may consist of a single program, such as Microsoft's notepad for writing and editing a simple text. It may also consist of a collection of programs, often called a software package, which work together to accomplish a task, such as a spreadsheet package. Commonly used Application software's are as:

a. **Word Processing:** Word processing software is used to manipulate a text document, such as a resume or a report. You typically enter text by typing, and the software provides tools for copying, deleting and various types of formatting. Some of the functions of word processing software include:
    i.   Creating, editing, saving and printing documents.
    ii. Copying, pasting, moving and deleting text within a document.
    iii. Formatting text, such as font type, bolding, underlining or italicizing.
    iv. Creating and editing tables.
    v.   Inserting elements from other software, such as illustrations or photographs.

vi.   Correcting spelling and grammar.

b. **Spreadsheet:** Spreadsheet software is a software application capable of organizing, storing and analyzing data in tabular form. The application can provide digital simulation of paper accounting worksheets. They can also have multiple interacting sheets with data represented in text, numeric or in graphic form. With these capabilities, spreadsheet software has replaced many paper-based systems, especially in the business world. Originally developed as an aid for accounting and bookkeeping tasks, spreadsheets are now widely used in other contexts where tabular lists can be used, modified and collaborated. Spreadsheet software is also known as a spreadsheet program or spreadsheet application.

c. **Database:** Database software is a software program or utility used for creating, editing and maintaining database files and records. This type of software allows users to store data in the form of structured fields, tables and columns, which can then be retrieved directly and/or through programmatic access. Database software is also known as database management software (DBMS). Database software is primarily used to store and manage data/databases, typically in a structured format. It generally provides a graphical interface that allows users to create, edit and manage data fields and records in a tabular or organized form. The data/database stored using this software can be retrieved in a raw or report-based format.

d. **Educational software:** Educational software is a term used for any computer software which is made for any educational purpose. It encompasses different ranges from language learning software to classroom management software to reference software, etc. The purpose of all this software is to make some part of education more effective and efficient.

e. **Entertainment software:** Entertainment software is any software that supports a hobby or provides a form of amusement. Entertainment software includes video games, videos and any other software that a user feels is enjoyable.

Firmware:

Firmware is a software program permanently etched into a hardware device such as a keyboards, hard drive, BIOS, or video card. It is programmed to give permanent instructions to communicate with other devices and perform functions like basic input/output tasks. Firmware is typically stored in the flash ROM (read only memory) of a hardware device. It can be erased and rewritten. Firmware was originally designed for high level software and could be changed without having to exchange the hardware for a newer device. Firmware also retains the basic instructions for hardware devices that make them operative. Without firmware, a hardware device would be non-functional.

Originally, firmware had read-only memory (ROM) and programmable read-only memory (PROM). It was designed to be permanent. Eventually PROM chips could be updated and were called erasable programmable read-only memory (EPROM). But EPROM was expensive, time consuming to update and challenging to use. Firmware eventually evolved from ROM to flash memory firmware; thus, it became easier to update and user friendly. There are levels of firmware:

Low Level Firmware: This is found in ROM, OTP/PROM and PLA structures. Low level firmware is often read-only memory and cannot be changed or updated. It is sometimes referred to as hardware.

High Level Firmware: This is used in flash memory for updates that is often considered as software.

Subsystems: These have their own fixed microcode embedded in flash chips, CPUs and LCD units. A subsystem is usually considered part of the hardware device as well as high level firmware.

BIOS, modems and video cards are usually easy to update. But firmware in storage devices usually gets overlooked; there are no standardized systems for updating firmware. Fortunately, storage devices do not need to be updated often.

Open-source software:

Open-source software is software with source code that anyone can inspect, modify, and enhance.

"Source code" is the part of software that most computer users don't ever see; it's the code computer programmers can manipulate to change how a piece of software—a "program" or "application"—works. Programmers who have access to a computer program's source code can improve that program by adding features to it or fixing parts that don't always work correctly.

Proprietary software:

Proprietary software is any software that is copyrighted and bears limits against use, distribution and modification that are imposed by its publisher, vendor or developer. Proprietary software remains the property of its owner/creator and is used by end-users/organizations under predefined conditions.

Proprietary software may also be called closed-source software or commercial software.

Difference between Open-source Software and Proprietary Software:

S.No.	OPEN-SOURCE SOFTWARE	PROPRIETARY SOFTWARE
01	Open-source software is computer software whose source code is available openly on the internet and programmers can modify it to add new features and capabilities without any cost.	Proprietary software is computer software where the source codes are publicly not available only the company which has created can modify it.
02	Here the software is developed and tested through open collaboration.	Here the software is developed and tested by the individual or organization by which it is owned not by the public.
03	Users can get open software free of charge.	Users must have to pay to get the proprietary software.

04	In open-source software the source code is public.	In proprietary software, the source code is protected.
05	It is more flexible and provides more freedom which encourages innovation.	It is not much flexible so there is a very limited innovation scope with the restrictions.
06	Users do not need to have any authenticated license to use this software.	Users need to have a valid and authenticated license to use this software.
07	Limited Intellectual Property Protections	Full Intellectual Property Protections
08	Examples are Android, Linux, Firefox, Open Office, GIMP, VLC Media player, etc.	Examples are Windows, macOS, Internet Explorer, Google Earth, Microsoft Office, Adobe Flash Player, Skype, etc.
09	Usually Developed and Maintained by non-profit organizations.	Usually Developed and Maintained by for-profit entities.

Basic Techniques to build a software:

Algorithm: The word "algorithm" relates to the name of the mathematician Al-khowarizmi, which means a procedure or a technique. Software Engineer commonly uses an algorithm for planning and solving the problems. An algorithm is a sequence of steps to solve a particular problem or algorithm is an ordered set of unambiguous steps that produces a result and terminates in a finite time

Algorithm has the following characteristics

   i.   Input: An algorithm may or may not require input

   ii.   Output: Each algorithm is expected to produce at least one result

   iii.   Definiteness: Each instruction must be clear and unambiguous.

   iv.   Finiteness: If the instructions of an algorithm are executed, the algorithm should terminate after finite number of steps

The algorithm and flowchart include following three types of control structures.

1. Sequence: In the sequence structure, statements are placed one after the other and the execution takes place starting from up to down.

2. Branching (Selection): In branch control, there is a condition and according to a condition, a decision of either TRUE or FALSE is achieved. In the case of TRUE, one of the two branches are explored; but in the case of FALSE condition, the other alternative is

taken. Generally, the 'IF-THEN' is used to represent branch control.

3.   Loop (Repetition): The Loop or Repetition allows a statement(s) to be executed repeatedly based on certain loop condition e.g. WHILE, FOR loops.

We can write an algorithm for adding two numbers as:

Step-1 Start

Step-2 Input first number say A

Step-3 Input second number say B

Step-4 SUM = A + B

Step-5 Display SUM

Step-6 Stop.

Flowchart: The first design of flowchart goes back to 1945 which was designed by John Von Neumann. Unlike an algorithm, Flowchart uses different symbols to design a solution to a problem. It is another commonly used programming tool. By looking at a Flowchart-one can understand the operations and sequence of operations performed in a system. Flowchart is often considered as a blueprint of a design used for solving a specific problem. Flowchart is diagrammatic /Graphical representation of sequence of steps to solve a problem. To draw a flowchart following standard symbols are use:

Symbol	Name	Function
	Process	Indicates any type of internal operation inside the Processor or Memory
	input/output	Used for any Input / Output (I/O) operation. Indicates that the computer is to obtain data or output results
	Decision	Used to ask a question that can be answered in a binary format (Yes/No, True/False)
	Connector	Allows the flowchart to be drawn without intersecting lines or without a reverse flow.
	Predefined Process	Used to invoke a subroutine or an Interrupt program.
	Terminal	Indicates the starting or ending of the program, process, or interrupt program
	Flow Lines	Shows direction of flow.

Example of flowchart

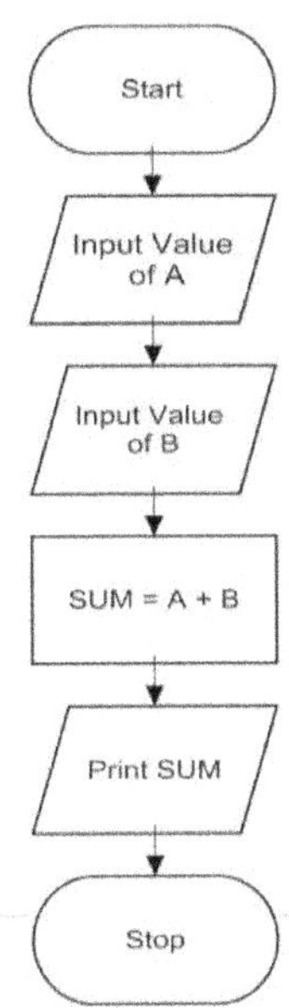

Pseudocode: Pseudocode is a simple way of writing programming code in English. Pseudocode is not actual programming language. It uses short phrases to write code for programs before you actually create it in a specific language. Once you know what the program is about and how it will function, then you can use pseudocode to create statements to achieve the required results for your program.

Pseudocode makes creating programs easier. Programs can be complex and long; preparation is the key. For years, flowcharts were used to map out programs before writing one line of code in a language. However, they were difficult to modify and with the advancement of programming languages, it was difficult to display all parts of a program with a flowchart. It is challenging to find a mistake without understanding the complete flow of a program. That is where pseudocode becomes more appealing.

To use pseudocode, all you do is write what you want your program to say in English. Pseudocode allows you to translate your statements into any language because there are no special commands and it is not standardized. Writing out programs before you code can enable you to better organize and see where you may have left out needed parts in your programs. All you have to do is write it out in your own words in short statements. Let's look at some examples.

Examples of Pseudocode

Let's review an example of pseudocode to create a program to add 2 numbers together and then display the result.

Start Program

Enter two numbers, A, B

Add the numbers together

Print Sum

End Program

Source code

Source code is any code, with or without comments, created by a human in a programming language typed in plain text, that has been executed and translated into binary by a computer and produced a non-error output, whether desirable or not. For example, you may have thought that system-generated code could be considered a source, but strictly speaking source code must be written by a human. Moreover, you may not have realized that source code must be successfully executed at least once. If not, it's just draft code. Finally, it's important to note that the execution must have produced a non-error output. In the case of an error, it's still just a draft. Moreover, even if the non-error output is undesirable, we consider the text source code. It simply needs to be fixed. Source code is also known as computer code.

Types of Source Code

The types of source code are:

Compiled source code

Interpreted source code

Computer (or operating system) source code

Software program source code

Software feature source code

Example

```c
int main()
{
    //declare num1 and num2 to hold the given numbers
    int num1, num2;
    //Taking the input
    scanf("%d %d", &num1, &num2);
    //Calculating the sum of num1 and num2
    int sum = num1 + num2;
    //Printing the addition of two numbers in C
    printf("The sum of the given numbers is: %d", sum);
    return 0;
}
```

Input

45

25

Output

The sum of the given numbers is: 70

Programming solving approaches

In the world of programming, algorithms take the prime spotlight. These complex mathematical and computational designs are used to find solutions to even more complex programming issues. Here we use two approaches those are as:

The Top-Down Approach

The Bottom-Up Approach

1. **The Top-Down Approach:** In this approach, a complex algorithm is broken down into smaller fragments, better known as 'modules.' These modules are then further broken down into smaller fragments until they can no longer be fragmented. This process is called 'modularization.' However, during the modularization process, you must always maintain the integrity and originality of the algorithm. Moreover, a top-down approach is more suitable when the software needs to be designed from scratch and very specific details are unknown. By breaking a bigger problem into smaller fragments, the top-down approach minimizes the complications usually incurred while designing algorithms. Furthermore, in this approach, each function in a code is unique and works independently of other functions. The top-down approach is heavily used in the C programming language.

Advantages: -

- ❖ Each module of code is to be tested separately.

- ❖ Breaking a problem down into smaller chunks makes it far easier to understand, solve and manage.

- ❖ Testing and debugging are efficient and easier.

❖ Project implementation is smoother and shorter.

Drawbacks: -

❖ Specification tends to change over time and in a top-down approach, all decisions made from the beginning of the project depend directly or indirectly on the high-level specification.

❖ In Dynamic Programming, the top-down approach is slow as compared to the bottom-up approach, as it involves recursion.

2. **The Bottom-Up Approach:** Contrary to the top-down approach, bottom-up programming focuses on designing an algorithm by beginning at the very basic level and building up as it goes. In this approach, the modules are designed individually and are then integrated together to form a complete algorithmic design. Moreover, the bottom-up approach is more suitable when a system needs to be created from some existing components. So, in this method, each and every module is built and tested at an individual level (unit testing) prior to integrating them to build a concrete solution. The unit testing is performed by leveraging specific low-level functions.

Advantages: -

❖ Test conditions are easier to create.

❖ Observation of test results is easier.

- ❖ Contains less redundancy due to the presence of data encapsulation and data-hiding.

- ❖ Reusability of the code.

Drawbacks: -

- ❖ In the Bottom-Up approach, we solve all sub-problems (even though some of the solutions of the subproblems aren't needed to solve), which requires additional calculations.

- ❖ In the Bottom-Up approach, sometimes it is difficult to identify the overall functionality of the system in the initial stages.

The Role of Algorithms in Computing

- The word Algorithm means "a process or set of rules to be followed in calculations or other problem-solving operations". Therefore, Algorithm refers to a set of rules/instructions that step-by-step define how a work is to be executed upon in order to get the expected results.

- Algorithms are at the core of most techniques used in contemporary computers alongside other technologies.

- An algorithm is an abstraction of a program to be executed on a physical machine (model of Computation).

Algorithm Design Technique

- <u>Strategy or paradigm</u> — General approach to solve program algorithmically

- <u>Brute Force</u> — Straight forward technique with naïve approach

- <u>Divide and conquer</u> — problem is divided into smaller instances

- <u>Decrease and conquer</u> — Instance size is decreased to solve the problem

- <u>Transform and conquer</u> — Instance is modified and then solved

- <u>Dynamic Programming</u> — Results of smaller, reoccurring instances are obtained to solve problem

- <u>Greedy Technique</u> — Solve the problem by making locally optimal decisions

Analysis of Algorithm

- <u>Time Efficiency</u> — Indicates how fasts algorithm runs

- <u>Space Efficiency</u> — How much extra memory the algorithm needs to complete its execution

- <u>Simplicity</u> — Generating sequence of instructions which are easy to understand

- <u>Generality</u> — Range of inputs it can accept.

Practical applications of algorithms:

- The Internet without which it is difficult to imagine a day is the result of clever and efficient algorithms. With the aid of these algorithms, various sites on the Internet are able to manage and manipulate this large volume of data. Finding good routes on which the data will travel and using search engine to find pages on which particular information is present.

- Another great milestone is the Human Genome Project which has great progress towards the goal of identification of the 100000 genes in human DNA, determining the sequences of the 3 billion chemical base pairs that make up the human DNA, storing this huge amount of information in databases, and developing tools for data analysis. Each of these steps required sophisticated and efficient algorithms.

- The day-to-day *electronic commerce* activities is hugely dependent on our personal information such as credit/debit card numbers, passwords, bank statements, OTPs and so on. The core technologies used include public-key cryptocurrency and digital signatures which are based on numerical algorithms and number theory.

- The approach of linear programming is also one such technique which is widely used like

    - In manufacturing and other commercial enterprises where resources need to be allocated scarcely in the most beneficial way.

    - Or a institution may want to determine where to spend money buying advertising in order to maximize the chances of their institution to grow.

- Shortest path algorithm also has an extensive use as

    - In a transportation firm such as a trucking or railroad company, may have financial interest in finding shortest path through a road or rail network because taking shortest path result in lower labour or fuel costs.

- Or a routing node on the Internet may need to find the shortest path through the network in order to route a message quickly.

- Even an application that does not require algorithm content at the application level relies heavily on algorithms as the application depends on hardware, GUI, networking or object orientation and all of these make an extensive use of algorithms.

Analysis of Algorithm

In theoretical analysis of algorithms, it is common to estimate their complexity in the asymptotic sense, i.e., to estimate the complexity function for arbitrarily large input. The term **"analysis of algorithms"** was coined by Donald Knuth.

Algorithm analysis is an important part of computational complexity theory, which provides theoretical estimation for the required resources of an algorithm to solve a specific computational problem. Most algorithms are designed to work with inputs of arbitrary length. Analysis of algorithms is the determination of the amount of time and space resources required to execute it.

Usually, the efficiency or running time of an algorithm is stated as a function relating the input length to the number of steps, known as **time complexity**, or volume of memory, known as **space complexity**.

The Need for Analysis

In this chapter, we will discuss the need for analysis of algorithms and how to choose a better algorithm for a particular problem as one computational problem can be solved by different algorithms.

By considering an algorithm for a specific problem, we can begin to develop pattern recognition so that similar types of problems can be solved by the help of this algorithm.

Algorithms are often quite different from one another, though the objective of these algorithms are the same. For example, we know that a set of numbers can be sorted using different algorithms. Number of comparisons performed by one algorithm may vary with others for the same input. Hence, time complexity of those algorithms may differ. At the same time, we need to calculate the memory space required by each algorithm.

Analysis of algorithm is the process of analyzing the problem-solving capability of the algorithm in terms of the time and size required (the size of memory for storage while implementation). However, the main concern of analysis of algorithms is the required time or performance. Generally, we perform the following types of analysis −

- **Worst-case** − The maximum number of steps taken on any instance of size **a**.

- **Best-case** − The minimum number of steps taken on any instance of size **a**.

- **Average case** − An average number of steps taken on any instance of size **a**.

- **Amortized** − A sequence of operations applied to the input of size **a** averaged over time.

To solve a problem, we need to consider time as well as space complexity as the program may run on a system where memory is limited but adequate space is available or may be vice-versa. In this context, if we compare **bubble sort** and **merge sort**. Bubble sort does not require additional memory, but merge sort requires additional space. Though time complexity of bubble sort is higher compared to merge sort, we may need to apply bubble sort if the program needs to run in an environment, where memory is very limited.

Computer Languages:

We are aware with the term language. It is a system of communication between two persons. Some of the basic natural languages that we are familiar with are English, Hindi, Oriya, etc. These are the languages used to communicate among various categories of persons. But how will you communicate with your computer. Your computer will not understand any of these natural languages for transfer of data and instruction. So, there are computer-programming languages specially developed so that you could pass your data and instructions to the computer to do specific job. You must have heard names like FORTRAN, BASIC, COBOL, etc. These are programming languages. So, instructions for performing a task are written in a particular computer programming language based on the type of job. As an example, for scientific application FORTRAN and C languages are used. On the other hand, COBOL is used mainly for business application.

There are two major types of programming languages.

1. Low Level Languages
2. High Level Languages

Low level languages: The term low level means closeness to the way in which the machine has been built. Low Level languages are machine oriented and require extensive knowledge of computer hardware and its configuration. The low-level languages are:

a. **Machine Language:** Machine Language is the language of the computer and is the only language that is directly understood by the computer. We also call it machine code and it is written as strings of 1's and 0's. It is on this basis that the computer is designed. When this sequence of codes is fed to the computer, it recognizes the codes and converts it in to electrical signals needed to run it. For example, a program instruction may look like this:

$$1011000111101$$

It is not an easy language for you to learn because of its complexity as it consists of 1's and 0's. It is most efficient for the computer as the instructions are directly executed. It is considered to the first-generation language. It is also difficult to debug the program written in this language.

Advantage:

i.   The only advantage is that program of machine language run very.

ii. Fast because no translation program is required for the CPU.

Disadvantages:

i. It is very difficult to program in machine language. The programmer has to know details of hardware to write program.
ii. Machine language is hardware dependent.
iii. The programmer has to remember a lot of codes to write a program, which results in program errors.
iv. It is difficult to debug the program.
b. **Assembly Language:** It is the first step to improve the programming structure. In this language, the machine codes comprising of 1'sand 0's are substituted by symbolic codes (called mnemonic codes) to improve their understanding. The set of symbols and letters forms the assembly language and a translator program (called Assembler) is required to translate the programs written in assembly language into machine language for execution by the computer. It is considered to be a second-generation language.

Advantages:

i. The symbolic programming of Assembly Language is easier to understand and saves a lot of time and effort of the programmer.
ii. It is relatively easier to correct errors and modify program instructions.
iii. Assembly Language has almost the same efficiency of execution as the machine level language because this is one-to-one translator between assembly language program and its corresponding machine language program.

Disadvantages:

a. One of the major disadvantages is that assembly language is machine dependent. A program written for one computer might not run-on other computers with different hardware configuration.

High Level Languages: You know that assembly language and machine language require extensive knowledge of computer hardware. To overcome this limitation, a user writes the instructions in English like sentences to perform the logic of the problem irrespective of the type of computer you are using. The language used for this is referred to as high-level language. High-level languages are simple language that use English and mathematical symbols like +, -, %, /, etc. for its program construction. You should know that any higher-level language has to be converted to machine language for the computer to understand. Higher-level languages are problem-oriented languages because the instructions are suitable for solving a particular problem. For example, COBOL (Common Business Oriented Language) is mostly suitable for business-oriented language where there is very little processing and huge output. There are mathematical oriented languages like FORTRAN (Formula Translation) and BASIC (Beginners All-purpose Symbolic Instructions Code) where very large processing is required. Thus, a problem-oriented language is designed in such a way that its instruction may be written more like the language of the problem. For example, businessmen use business term and scientists use scientific terms in their respective languages.

Advantages of High-Level Languages

Higher-level languages have a major advantage over machine and assembly languages that higher-level languages are easy to learn and use. It is because that they are similar to the languages used by us in our day-to-day life. The programs can easily be debugged and are machine independent.

4GL: A fourth generation (programming) language (4GL) is a grouping of programming languages that attempt to get closer than 3GLs to human language, form of thinking and conceptualization.

4GLs are designed to reduce the overall time, effort and cost of software development. The main domains and families of 4GLs are: database queries, report generators, data manipulation, analysis and reporting, screen painters and generators, GUI creators, mathematical optimization, web development and general-purpose languages.

Also known as a 4th generation language, a domain specific language, or a high productivity language

Translator: A translator is a programming language processor that converts a computer program from one language to another. It takes a program written in source code and converts it into machine code. It discovers and identifies the error during translation.

Purpose of Translator: It translates a high-level language program into a machine language program that the central processing unit (CPU) can understand. It also detects errors in the program.

Different Types of Translators

There are 3 different types of translators as follows:

Compiler

A compiler is a translator used to convert high-level programming language to low-level programming language. It converts the whole program in one session and reports errors detected after the conversion. The compiler takes time to do its work as it translates high-level code to lower-level code all at once and then saves it to memory.

A compiler is processor-dependent and platform-dependent. But it has been addressed by a special compiler, a cross-compiler and a source-to-source compiler. Before choosing a compiler, the user has to identify first the Instruction Set Architecture (ISA), the operating system (OS), and the programming language that will be used to ensure that it will be compatible.

Interpreter

Just like a compiler, is a translator used to convert high-level programming language to low-level programming language. It converts the program one at a time and reports errors detected at once while doing the conversion. With this, it is easier to detect errors than in a compiler. An interpreter is faster than a compiler as it immediately executes the code upon reading the code.

It is often used as a debugging tool for software development as it can execute a single line of code at a time. An interpreter is also more portable than a compiler as it is not processor-dependent, you can work between hardware architectures.

Assembler

An assembler is a translator used to translate assembly language to machine language. It is like a compiler for the assembly language but interactive like an interpreter. Assembly language is difficult to understand as it is a low-level programming language. An assembler translates a low-level language, an assembly language to an even lower-level language, which is the machine code. The machine code can be directly understood by the CPU.

Examples of Translators

Here are some examples of translators per type:

Translator	Examples
Compiler	Microsoft Visual Studio GNU Compiler Collection (GCC) Common Business Oriented Language (COBOL)
Interpreter	OCaml List Processing (LISP) Python
Assembler	Fortran Assembly Program (FAP) Macro Assembly Program (MAP) Symbolic Optimal Assembly Program (SOAP)

Database:

A database is a systematic collection of data. They support electronic storage and manipulation of data. Databases make data management easy.

Let us discuss a database example: An online telephone directory uses a database to store data of people, phone numbers, and other contact details. Your electricity service provider uses a database to manage billing, client-related issues, handle fault data, etc.

Let us also consider Facebook. It needs to store, manipulate, and present data related to members, their friends, member activities, messages, advertisements, and a lot more. We can provide a countless number of examples for the usage of databases.

Types of Databases

Here are some popular types of databases.

Distributed databases:

A distributed database is a type of database that has contributions from the common database and information captured by local computers. In this type of database system, the data is not in one place and is distributed at various organizations.

Relational databases:

This type of database defines database relationships in the form of tables. It is also called Relational DBMS, which is the most popular DBMS type in the market. Database example of the

RDBMS system include MySQL, Oracle, and Microsoft SQL Server database.

Object-oriented databases:

This type of computers database supports the storage of all data types. The data is stored in the form of objects. The objects to be held in the database have attributes and methods that define what to do with the data. PostgreSQL is an example of an object-oriented relational DBMS.

Centralized database:

It is a centralized location, and users from different backgrounds can access this data. This type of computers databases store application procedures that help users access the data even from a remote location.

Open-source databases:

This kind of database stored information related to operations. It is mainly used in the field of marketing, employee relations, customer service, of databases.

Cloud databases:

A cloud database is a database which is optimized or built for such a virtualized environment. There are so many advantages of a cloud database, some of which can pay for storage capacity and bandwidth. It also offers scalability on-demand, along with high availability.

Data warehouses:

Data Warehouse is to facilitate a single version of truth for a company for decision making and forecasting. A Data warehouse is an information system that contains historical and commutative data from single or multiple sources. Data Warehouse concept simplifies the reporting and analysis process of the organization.

NoSQL databases:

NoSQL database is used for large sets of distributed data. There are a few big data performance problems that are effectively handled by relational databases. This type of computers database is very efficient in analyzing large-size unstructured data.

Graph databases:

A graph-oriented database uses graph theory to store, map, and query relationships. These kinds of computers databases are mostly used for analyzing interconnections. For example, an organization can use a graph database to mine data about customers from social media.

OLTP databases:

OLTP another database type which able to perform fast query processing and maintaining data integrity in multi-access environments.

Personal database:

A personal database is used to store data stored on personal computers that are smaller and easily manageable. The data is mostly used by the same department of the company and is accessed by a small group of people.

Multimodal database:

The multimodal database is a type of data processing platform that supports multiple data models that define how the certain knowledge and information in a database should be organized and arranged.

Document/JSON database:

In a document-oriented database, the data is kept in document collections, usually using the XML, JSON, BSON formats. One record can store as much data as you want, in any data type (or types) you prefer.

Hierarchical:

This type of DBMS employs the "parent-child" relationship of storing data. Its structure is like a tree with nodes representing records and branches representing fields. The windows registry used in Windows XP is a hierarchical database example.

Network DBMS:

This type of DBMS supports many-to-many relations. It usually results in complex database structures. RDM Server is an example of database management system that implements the network model.

Database Components

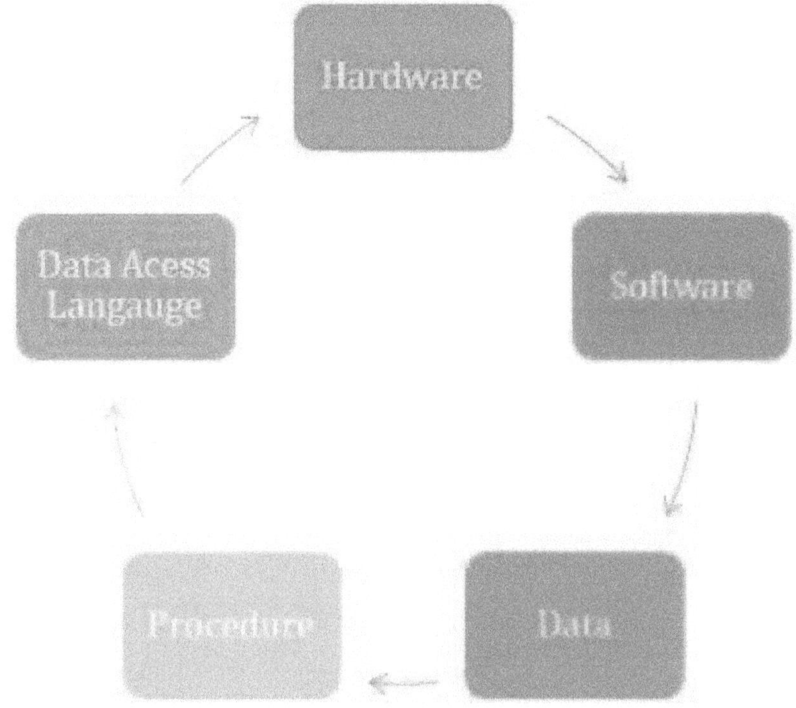

Database Components

There are five main components of a database:

Hardware:

The hardware consists of physical, electronic devices like computers, I/O devices, storage devices, etc. This offers the interface between computers and real-world systems.

Software:

This is a set of programs used to manage and control the overall database. This includes the database software itself, the Operating System, the network software used to share the data among users, and the application programs for accessing data in the database.

Data:

Data is a raw and unorganized fact that is required to be processed to make it meaningful. Data can be simple at the same time unorganized unless it is organized. Generally, data comprises facts, observations, perceptions, numbers, characters, symbols, images, etc.

Procedure:

Procedure are a set of instructions and rules that help you to use the DBMS. It is designing and running the database using documented methods, which allows you to guide the users who operate and manage it.

Database Access Language:

Database Access language is used to access the data to and from the database, enter new data, update already existing data, or retrieve required data from DBMS. The user writes some specific commands in a database access language and submits these to the database.

Database Management System (DBMS)

Database Management System (DBMS) is a collection of programs that enable its users to access databases, manipulate data, report, and represent data. It also helps to control access to the database. Database Management Systems are not a new concept and, as such, had been first implemented in the 1960s.

Charles Bachman's Integrated Data Store (IDS) is said to be the first DBMS in history. With time database, technologies evolved a lot, while usage and expected functionalities of databases increased immensely.

History of Database Management System

Here, are the important landmarks from the history:

- 1960 – Charles Bachman designed first DBMS system.

- 1970 – Codd introduced IBM'S Information Management System (IMS).

- 1976 – Peter Chen coined and defined the Entity-relationship model also known as the ER model.

- 1980 – Relational model becomes a widely accepted database component.

- 1985 – Object-oriented DBMS develops.

- 1990 – Incorporation of object-orientation in relational DBMS.

- 1991 – Microsoft ships MS access, a personal DBMS and that displaces all other personal DBMS products.

- 1995 – First Internet database applications.

- 1997 – XML applied to database processing. Many vendors begin to integrate XML into DBMS products.

Advantages of DBMS

- DBMS offers a variety of techniques to store & retrieve data.

- DBMS serves as an efficient handler to balance the needs of multiple applications using the same data.

- Uniform administration procedures for data.

- Application programmers never exposed to details of data representation and storage.

- A DBMS uses various powerful functions to store and retrieve data efficiently.

- Offers Data Integrity and Security.

- The DBMS implies integrity constraints to get a high level of protection against prohibited access to data.

- A DBMS schedules concurrent access to the data in such a manner that only one user can access the same data at a time.

- Reduced Application Development Time.

Disadvantage of DBMS

DBMS may offer plenty of advantages but, it has certain flaws-

- Cost of Hardware and Software of a DBMS is quite high which increases the budget of your organization.

- Most database management systems are often complex systems, so the training for users to use the DBMS is required.

- In some organizations, all data is integrated into a single database which can be damaged because of electric failure or database is corrupted on the storage media.

- Use of the same program at a time by many users sometimes lead to the loss of some data.

- DBMS can't perform sophisticated calculations.

Application of DBMS

There are different fields where a database management system is utilized. Following are a few applications which utilize the information base administration framework –

1. **Railway Reservation System –**
    In the rail route reservation framework, the information base is needed to store the record or information of ticket appointments, status about train's appearance, and flight. Additionally, if trains get late, individuals become acquainted with it through the information base update.

2. **Library Management System –**
    There are lots of books in the library so; it is difficult to store the record of the relative multitude of books in a register or duplicate. Along these lines, the data set administration framework (DBMS) is utilized to keep up all the data identified with the name of the book, issue date, accessibility of the book, and its writer.

3. **Banking –**
    Database the executive's framework is utilized to store the exchange data of the client in the information base.

4. **Education Sector –**
    Presently, assessments are led online by numerous schools and colleges. They deal with all assessment information through the data set administration framework (DBMS). In spite of that understudy's

enlistments subtleties, grades, courses, expense, participation, results, and so forth all the data is put away in the information base.

5. **Credit card exchanges –**
The database Management framework is utilized for buying on charge cards and age of month-to-month proclamations.

6. **Social Media Sites –**
We all utilization of online media sites to associate with companions and to impart our perspectives to the world. Every day, many people group pursue these online media accounts like Pinterest, Facebook, Twitter, and Google in addition to. By the utilization of the data set administration framework, all the data of clients are put away in the information base and, we become ready to interface with others.

7. **Broadcast communications –**
Without DBMS any media transmission organization can't think. The Database the executive's framework is fundamental for these organizations to store the call subtleties and month to month post-paid bills in the information base.

8. **Account –**
The information base administration framework is utilized for putting away data about deals, holding and

acquisition of monetary instruments, for example, stocks and bonds in a data set.

9. **Online Shopping** –
These days, web-based shopping has become a major pattern. Nobody needs to visit the shop and burn through their time. Everybody needs to shop through web-based shopping sites, (for example, Amazon, Flipkart, Snapdeal) from home. So, all the items are sold and added uniquely with the assistance of the information base administration framework (DBMS). Receipt charges, instalments, buy data these are finished with the assistance of DBMS.

10. **Human Resource Management** –
Big firms or organizations have numerous specialists or representatives working under them. They store data about worker's compensation, assessment, and work with the assistance of an information base administration framework (DBMS).

11. **Manufacturing** –
Manufacturing organizations make various kinds of items and deal them consistently. To keep the data about their items like bills, acquisition of the item, amount, inventory network the executives, information base administration framework (DBMS) is utilized.

12. **Airline Reservation System** – This framework is equivalent to the railroad reservation framework. This framework additionally utilizes an information base administration framework to store the records of flight take-off, appearance, and defer status.

Data

In general, data is a distinct piece of information that is gathered and translated for some purpose. Data can be available in different forms, such as bits and bytes stored in electronic memory, numbers or text on pieces of paper, or facts stored in a person's mind.

Big Data

Big Data is defined as the Data which are very large in size. Normally, we work on data of size MB (WordDoc, Excel) or maximum GB (Movies, Codes), but data in Petabytes, i.e., 10^{15}-byte size, is called Big Data. It is stated that almost 90% of today's data has been generated in the past 3 years. Big data sources include Telecom Companies, Weather stations, E-commerce sites, Share market, and many more.

Big Data can be structured, unstructured, and semi-structured that are being collected from different sources.

Now, let's discuss Structured Data and Unstructured Data.

Structured Data

The data which is to the point, factual, and highly organized is referred to as structured data. It is quantitative in nature, i.e., it is related to quantities that means it contains measurable numerical values like numbers, dates, and times.

Structured Data

13.

It is easy to search and analyze structured data. Structured data exists in a predefined format. Relational database consisting of tables with rows and columns is one of the best examples of structured data. Structured data generally exist in tables like excel files and Google Docs spreadsheets. The programming language SQL (structured query language) is used for managing the structured data. SQL is developed by IBM in the 1970s and majorly used to handle relational databases and warehouses.

Structured data is highly organized and understandable for machine language. Common applications of relational databases with structured data include sales transactions, Airline reservation systems, inventory control, and others.

Unstructured Data

All the unstructured files, log files, audio files, and image files are included in the unstructured data. Some organizations have much data available, but they did not know how to derive data value since the data is raw.

Unstructured data is the data that lacks any predefined model or format. It requires a lot of storage space, and it is hard to maintain security in it. It cannot be presented in a data model or schema. That's why managing, analyzing, or searching for unstructured data is hard. It resides in various different formats like text, images, audio and video files, etc. It is qualitative in nature and sometimes stored in a non-relational database or NO-SQL.

It is not stored in relational databases, so it is hard for computers and humans to interpret it. The limitations of unstructured data include the requirement of data science experts and specialized tools to manipulate the data.

The amount of unstructured data is much more than the structured or semi-structured data. Examples of human-generated unstructured data are Text files, Email, social media, media, mobile data, business applications, and others. The machine-generated unstructured data includes satellite images, scientific data, sensor data, digital surveillance, and many more.

Structured data v/s Unstructured data

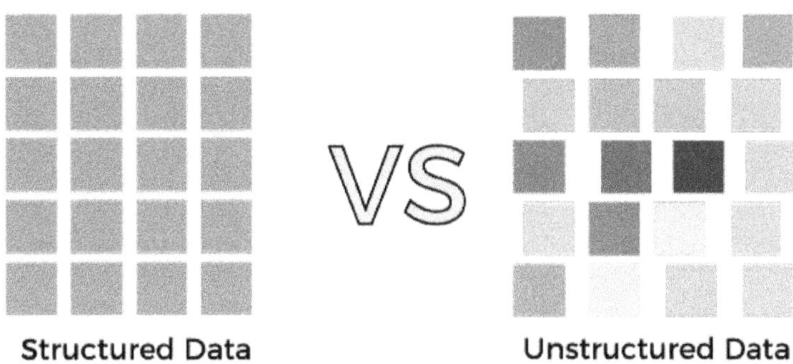

Let's see the comparison chart between structured and unstructured data. Here, we are tabulating the difference between both terms based on some characteristics.

On the basis of	Structured data	Unstructured data

Technology	It is based on a relational database.	It is based on character and binary data.
Flexibility	Structured data is less flexible and schema-dependent.	There is an absence of schema, so it is more flexible.
Scalability	It is hard to scale database schema.	It is more scalable.
Robustness	It is very robust.	It is less robust.
Performance	Here, we can perform a structured query that allows complex joining, so the performance is higher.	While in unstructured data, textual queries are possible, the performance is lower than semi-structured and structured data.
Nature	Structured data is quantitative, i.e., it consists of hard numbers or things that can be counted.	It is qualitative, as it cannot be processed and analyzed using conventional tools.
Format	It has a predefined format.	It has a variety of formats, i.e., it comes in a variety of shapes and sizes.

Analysis	It is easy to search.	Searching for unstructured data is more difficult.

Chapter 4: Networking and IT Trends

Networking:

Networking, also known as computer networking, is the practice of transporting and exchanging data between nodes over a shared medium in an information system. Networking comprises not only the design, construction and use of a network, but also the management, maintenance and operation of the network infrastructure, software and policies.

Computer networking enables devices and endpoints to be connected to each other on a local area network (LAN) or to a larger network, such as the internet or a private wide area network (WAN). This is an essential function for service providers, businesses and consumers worldwide to share resources, use or offer services, and communicate.

Communication:

Communication means the exchange of information or messages. When we talk with each other, we are exchanging information. Data communication can be defined as: "By using the transmission media, data or information is transmitted from one location to another is called data communication". For data communication, computers, telephones, and wireless devices that are linked in a network are used. Physical transfer of data over a point to point (communication connection between two nodes or end points) or point to multi-point (communication which is accomplished via distinct type of one-to-many connection) channel is called data transmission.

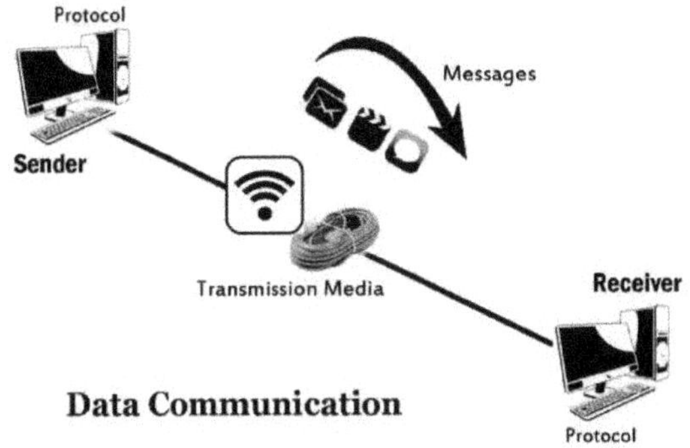

Data Communication

Basic elements of Communication: There are six Basic elements of Communication

1. Message
2. Sender
3. Receiver
4. Medium
5. Encoder
6. Decoder

1. **Message:** The message is the information or data that is communicated. It may consist of text, numbers, images, sound, video etc.

2. **Sender:** The computer or device that sends the data or messages is called sender. In data communication system, computer is usually used as a transmitter. It is also called sender. A sender may be computer, workstation, telephone, video camera etc.

3. **Receiver:** The device that receives the data or messages is called receiver. Receiver is also known as sink. The receiver can be a computer, workstation, printer or a fax machine.

4. **Medium:** The path through which data is sent or transmitted from one location to another is called communication channel. If the receiver and the sender are within a building, a wire may be the communication channel. If they are located at different locations, the channel may be the telephone lines, fibre optics, satellite or microwaves.

5. **Encoder:** The computer works with digital signals. The communication channels usually use analog signals. Therefore, to send data through a communication channel, the digital signals are encoded (or converted) into analog signals or into a form which can be transmitted through transmission medium. This is called encoding. The device that carries out this function is called encoder.

6. **Decoder:** The computer works with digital signals. The communication channels usually use analog signals. Therefore, to receive data from a communication channel, the coded analog signals or any other encoded form are converted back to digital signals. This is called decoding. The device that carries out this function is called decoder.

Transmission media:

A transmission medium is a physical path between the transmitter and the receiver i.e. it is the channel through which data is sent from one place to another. Transmission Media is broadly classified into the following types: -

a. Guided media
b. Unguided media

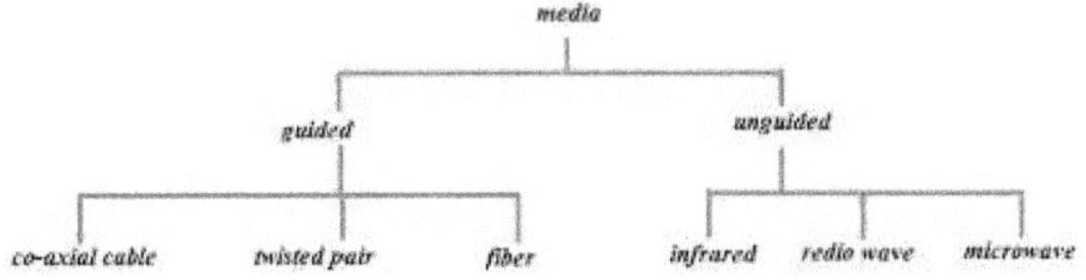

Guided Media: It is also referred to as Wired or Bounded transmission media. Signals being transmitted are directed and confined in a narrow pathway by using physical links. This type of media is High Speed, Secure and Used for comparatively shorter distances.

There are 3 major types of Guided Media:

a. **Coaxial Cable:** It has an outer plastic covering containing 2 parallel conductors each having a separate insulated protection cover. Coaxial cable transmits information in two modes: Baseband mode (dedicated cable bandwidth) and Broadband mode (cable bandwidth is split into separate ranges). Cable TVs and analog television networks widely use Coaxial cables.

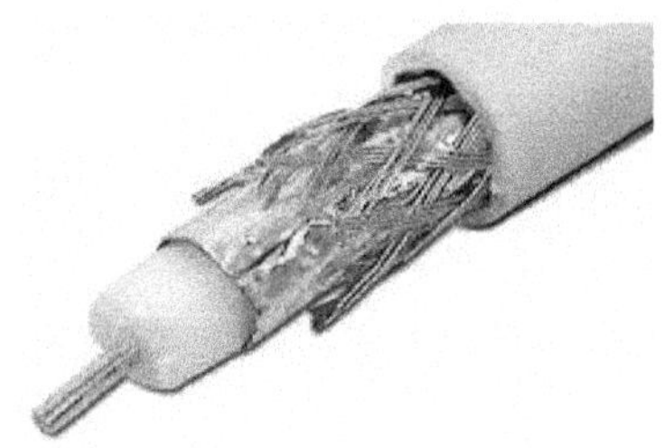

b. **Twisted Pair Cable:** It consists of 2 separately insulated conductor wires wound about each other. Generally, several such pairs are bundled together in a protective sheath. They are the most widely used Transmission Media. Twisted Pair is of two types:

Unshielded Twisted Pair (UTP): This type of cable has the ability to block interference and does not depend on a physical shield for this purpose. It is used for telephonic applications.

Shielded Twisted Pair (STP): This type of cable consists of a special jacket to block external interference. It is used in fast-data-rate Ethernet and in voice and data channels of telephone lines.

c. **Optical Fibre Cable:** It uses the concept of reflection of light through a core made up of glass or plastic. The core is surrounded by a less dense glass or plastic covering called the cladding. It is used for transmission of large volumes of data.

Unguided Media: It is also referred to as Wireless or Unbounded transmission media. No physical medium is required for the transmission of electromagnetic signals. There are 3 major types of Unguided Media:

(i) **Infrared:** Infrared waves are used for very short distance communication. They cannot penetrate through obstacles. This prevents interference between systems. Frequency Range:300GHz – 400THz. It is used in TV remotes, wireless mouse, keyboard, printer, etc.

(ii) **Radio waves:** These are easy to generate and can penetrate through buildings. The sending and receiving antennas need not be aligned. Frequency Range:3KHz – 1GHz. AM and FM radios and cordless phones use Radio waves for transmission. These are further categorized as Terrestrial and Satellite.

(iii) **Microwaves:** It is a line-of-sight transmission i.e., the sending and receiving antennas need to be properly aligned with each other. The distance covered by the signal is directly proportional to the height of the antenna. Frequency Range:1GHz – 300GHz. These are majorly used for mobile phone communication and television distribution.

Modes of Communication:

There are three types of transmission mode

1. Simplex Mode
2. Half-Duplex Mode
3. Full-Duplex Mode

1. **Simplex Mode:** In Simplex mode, the communication is unidirectional, as on a one-way street. Only one of the two devices on a link can transmit, the other can only receive. The simplex mode can use the entire capacity of the channel to send data in one direction. Example: Keyboard and traditional monitors. The keyboard can only introduce input, the monitor can only give the output.

2. **Half-Duplex Mode:** In half-duplex mode, each station can both transmit and receive, but not at the same time. When one device is sending, the other can only receive, and vice versa. The half-duplex mode is used in cases where there is no need for communication in both direction at the same time. The entire capacity of the channel can be utilized for each direction. Example: Walkie- talkie in which message is sent one at a time and messages are sent in both the directions.

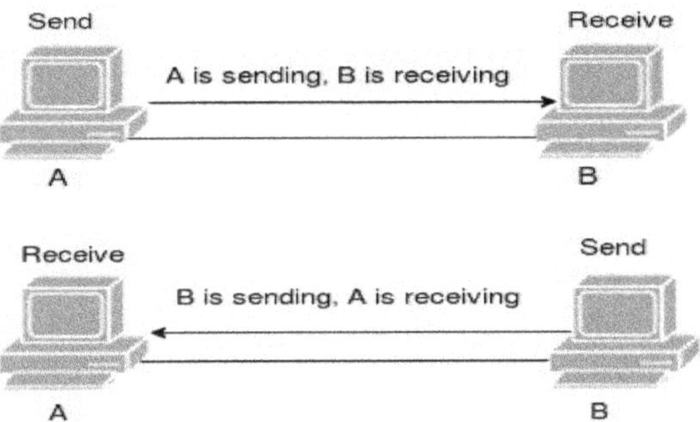

3. **Full-Duplex Mode:** In full-duplex mode, both stations can transmit and receive simultaneously. In fullduplex mode, signals going in one direction share the capacity of the link with signals going in other direction, this sharing can occur in two ways:

- Either the link must contain two physically separate transmission paths, one for sending and other for receiving.
- Or the capacity is divided between signals travelling in both directions.

Full-duplex mode is used when communication in both directions is required all the time. The capacity of the channel, however must be divided between the two directions. Example is Telephone Network in which there is communication between two persons by a telephone line, through which both can talk and listen at the same time.

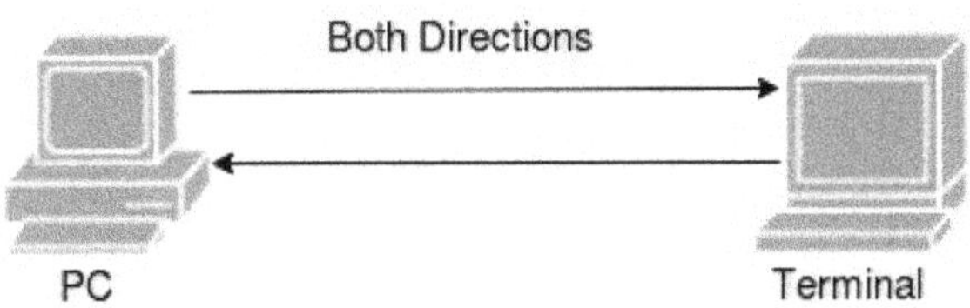

Network and its types:

Two devices are in network if a process in one device is able to exchange information with a process in another device. Networks are known as a medium of connections between nodes (set of devices) or computers. A network is consisting of group of computer systems, servers, networking devices are linked together to share resources, including a printer or a file server. The connections are established by using either cable media or wireless media.

Computer Networks fall into three classes regarding the size, distance and the structure namely:

a. LAN (Local Area Network)
b. MAN (Metropolitan Area Network)
c. WAN (Wide Area Network)

a. **LAN (Local Area Network):** A Local Area Network is a privately-owned computer network covering a small Networks geographical area, like a home, office, or groups of buildings e.g. a school Network. A LAN is used to connect the computers and other network devices so that the devices can communicate with each other to share the resources. The resources to be shared can be a hardware device like printer, software like an application program or data. The size of LAN is usually small. The various devices in LAN are connected to central devices called Hub or Switch using a cable.

Now-a-days LANs are being installed using wireless technologies. Such a system makes use of access point or APs to transmit and receive data. One of the computers in a network can become a server serving all the remaining computers called Clients. For example, a library will have a wired or wireless LAN Network for users to interconnect local networking devices e.g., printers and servers to connect to the internet. LAN offers high speed communication of data rates of 4 to 16 megabits per second (Mbps).

b. **MAN (Metropolitan Area Networks):** MAN stands for Metropolitan Area Networks is one of a number of types of networks. A MAN is a relatively new class of network. MAN is larger than a local area network and as its name implies, covers the area of a single city. MANs rarely extend beyond 100 KM and frequently comprise a combination of different hardware and transmission media. It can be single network such as a cable TV network, or it is a means of connecting a number of LANs into a larger network so that resources can be shared LAN to LAN as well as device to device.

A MAN can be created as a single network such as Cable TV Network, covering the entire city or a group of several Local Area Networks (LANs). It this way resource can be shared from LAN to LAN and from computer to computer also. MANs are usually owned by large organizations to interconnect its various branches across a city.

c. **WAN (Wide Area Networks):** A wide area network (WAN) is a telecommunication network. A wide area network is simply a LAN of LANs or Network of Networks. WANs connect LANs that may be on opposite sides of a building, across the country or around the world. WANS are characterized by the slowest data communication rates and the largest distances. WANs can be of two types: an enterprise WAN and Global

WAN. Computers connected to a Wide Area Networks are often connected through public networks, such as the telephone system. They can also be connected through leased lines or satellites. The largest WAN in existence is the Internet. Some segments of the Internet, like VPN based extranets, are also WANs in themselves. Finally, many WANs are corporate or research networks that utilize leased lines. Numerous WANs have been constructed, including public packet networks, large corporate networks, military networks, banking networks, stock brokerage networks, and airline reservation networks.

Networking devices

The term internetworking is a widely-used term for any hardware within networks that connect different network resources. Key devices that comprise a network are routers, bridges, repeaters and gateways.

All devices have separately installed scope features, per network requirements and scenarios. Some of these devices are

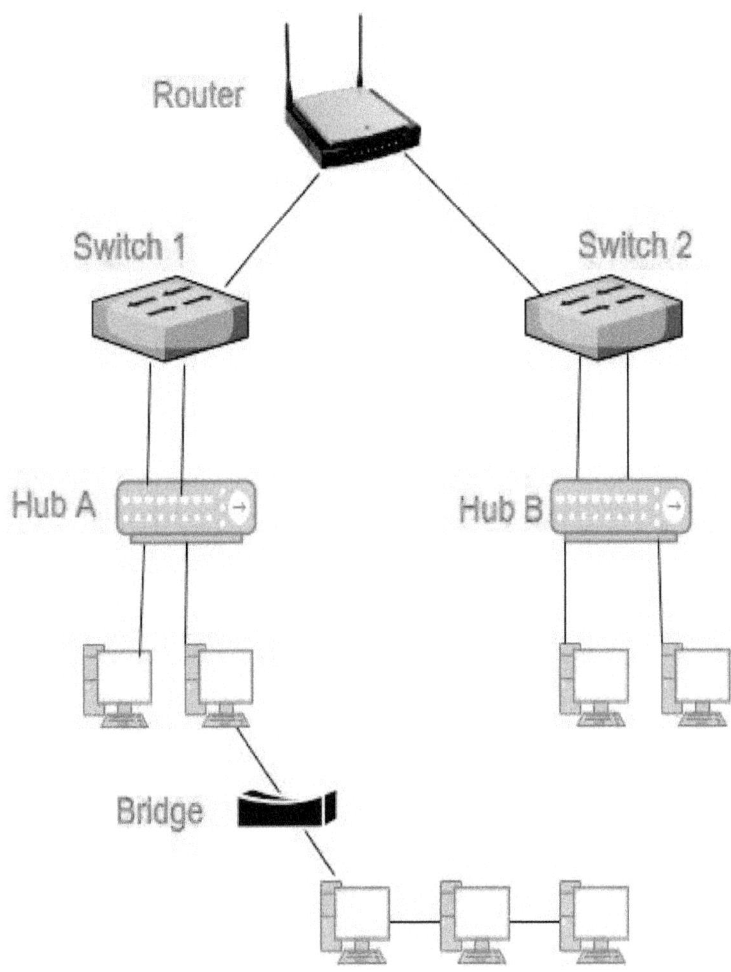

a) **Hub:** A hub is basically a multiport repeater. A hub connects multiple wires coming from different branches, for example, the connector in star topology which connects different stations. Hubs cannot filter data, so data packets are sent to all connected devices. In other words, collision domain of all hosts connected through Hub remains one. Also, they do not have intelligence to find out best path for data packets which leads to inefficiencies and wastage. There are two types of hubs:

❖ Active Hub: - These are the hubs which have their own power supply and can clean, boost and relay the signal along the network. It serves both as a repeater as well as wiring center. These are used to extend maximum distance between nodes.

❖ Passive Hub: - These are the hubs which collect wiring from nodes and power supply from active hub. These hubs relay signals onto the network without cleaning and boosting them and can't be used to extend distance between nodes.

b) **Switch:** A switch is a multi-port bridge with a buffer and a design that can boost its efficiency (large number of ports imply less traffic) and performance. Switch is data link layer device. Switch can perform error checking before forwarding data, that makes it very efficient as it does not forward packets that have errors and forward good packets selectively to correct port only. In other words, switch divides collision domain of hosts, but broadcast domain remains same.

c) **Router:** A router is a device like a switch that routes data packets based on their IP addresses. Router is mainly a Network Layer device. Routers normally connect LANs and WANs together and have a dynamically updating routing table based on which they make decisions on routing the data packets. Router divide broadcast domains of hosts connected through it.

d) **Bridge:** A bridge operates at data link layer. A bridge is a repeater, with add on functionality of filtering content by reading the MAC addresses of source and destination. It is also used for interconnecting two LANs working on the same protocol. It has a single input and single output port, thus making it a 2-port device. There are two types of Bridges:

- ❖ Transparent Bridges: These are the bridge in which the stations are completely unaware of the bridge's existence i.e. whether or not a bridge is added or deleted from the network, reconfiguration of the stations is unnecessary. These bridges make use of two processes i.e. bridge forwarding and bridge learning.
- ❖ Source Routing Bridges: In these bridges, routing operation is performed by source station and the frame specifies which route to follow. The hot can discover frame by sending a special frame called discovery frame, which spreads through the entire network using all possible paths to destination.

e) **Repeater:** A repeater operates at the physical layer. Its job is to regenerate the signal over the same network before the signal becomes too weak or corrupted so as to extend the length to which the signal can be transmitted over the same network. An important point to be noted about repeaters is that they do not amplify the signal. When the signal becomes weak, they copy the signal bit by bit and regenerate it at the original strength. It is a 2-port device.

f) **Gateway:** A gateway, as the name suggests, is a passage to connect two networks together that may work upon different networking models. They basically work as the messenger agents that take data from one system, interpret it, and transfer it to another system. Gateways are also called protocol converters and can operate at any network layer. Gateways are generally more complex than switch or router.

g) **Brouter:** It is also known as bridging router is a device which combines features of both bridge and router. It can work either at data link layer or at network layer. Working as router, it is capable of routing packets across networks and working as bridge, it is capable of filtering local area network traffic.

h) **Server:** A server is a computer program or device that provides a service to another computer program and its user, also known as the client. In a data center, the physical computer that a server program runs on is also frequently referred to as a server. That machine might be a dedicated server or it might be used for other purposes.

In the client/server programming model, a server program awaits and fulfills requests from client programs, which might be running in the same, or other computers. A given application in a computer might function as a client with requests for services from other programs and as a server of requests from other programs.

Virus:

A computer virus is a malicious program that self-replicates by copying itself to another program. In other words, the computer virus spreads by itself into other executable code or documents. The purpose of creating a computer virus is to infect vulnerable systems, gain admin control and steal user sensitive data. Hackers design computer viruses with malicious intent and prey on online users by tricking them.

One of the ideal methods by which viruses spread is through emails – opening the attachment in the email, visiting an infected website, clicking on an executable file, or viewing an infected advertisement can cause the virus to spread to your system. Besides that, infections also spread while connecting with already infected removable storage devices, such as USB drives. It is quite easy and simple for the viruses to sneak into a computer by dodging the defense systems. A successful breach can cause serious issues for the user such as infecting other resources or system software, modifying or deleting key functions or applications and copy/delete or encrypt data.

A computer virus operates in two ways. The first kind, as soon as it lands on a new computer, begins to replicate. The second type plays dead until the trigger kick starts the malicious code. In other words, the infected program needs to run to be executed. Therefore, it is highly significant to stay shielded by installing a robust antivirus program.

Types of Computer Viruses:

A computer virus is one type of malware that inserts its virus code to multiply itself by altering the programs and applications. The computer gets infected through the replication of malicious code. Computer viruses come in different forms to infect the system in different ways. Some of the most common viruses are:

a. Boot Sector Virus – This type of virus infects the master boot record and it is challenging and a complex task to remove this virus and often requires the system to be formatted. Mostly it spreads through removable media.

b. Direct Action Virus – This is also called non-resident virus, it gets installed or stays hidden in the computer memory. It stays attached to the specific type of files that it infects. It does not affect the user experience and system's performance.

c. Resident Virus – Unlike direct action viruses, resident viruses get installed on the computer. It is difficult to identify the virus and it is even difficult to remove a resident virus.

d. Multipartite Virus – This type of virus spreads through multiple ways. It infects both the boot sector and executable files at the same time.

e. Polymorphic Virus – These types of viruses are difficult to identify with a traditional anti-virus program. This is because the polymorphic viruses alter its signature pattern whenever it replicates.

f. Overwrite Virus – This type of virus deletes all the files that it infects. The only possible mechanism to remove is to delete the infected files and the end-user has to lose all the contents in it. Identifying the overwrite virus is difficult as it spreads through emails.

g. Spacefiller Virus – This is also called "Cavity Viruses". This is called so as they fill up the empty spaces between the code and hence does not cause any damage to the file.

h. File infectors: Few file infector viruses come attached with program files, such as .com or .exe files. Some file infector viruses infect any program for which execution is requested, including .sys, .ovl, .prg, and .mnu files. Consequently, when the particular program is loaded, the virus is also loaded.

i. Macro viruses: As the name suggests, the macro viruses particularly target macro language commands in applications like Microsoft Word. The same is implied on other programs too.

    In MS Word, the macros are keystrokes that are embedded in the documents or saved sequences for commands. The macro viruses are designed to add their malicious code to the genuine macro sequences in a Word file. However, as the years went by, Microsoft Word witnessed disabling of macros by default in more recent versions. Thus, the cybercriminals started to use social engineering schemes to target users. In the process, they trick the user and enable macros to launch the virus. Since macro viruses are making a comeback in the recent years, Microsoft quickly retaliated by adding a new feature in Office 2016. The feature enables security managers to selectively enable macro use. As a matter of fact, it can be enabled for trusted workflows and blocked if required across the organization.

j. Overwrite Viruses: The virus design purpose tends to vary and Overwrite Viruses are predominantly designed to destroy a file or application's data. As the name says it all, the virus after attacking the computer starts overwriting files with its own code. Not to be taken lightly, these viruses are more capable of targeting specific files or applications or systematically overwrite all files on an infected device. On the flipside, the overwrite virus is capable of installing a new code in the files or applications which programs them to spread the virus to additional files, applications, and systems.

k. Polymorphic Viruses: More and more cybercriminals are depending on the polymorphic virus. It is a malware type which has the ability to change or mutate its underlying code without changing its basic functions or features. This helps the virus on a computer or network to evade detection from many antimalware and threat detection products. Since virus removal programs depend on identifying signatures of malware, these viruses are carefully designed to escape detection and identification. When a security software detects a polymorphic virus, the virus modifies itself thereby, it is no longer detectable using the previous signature.

l. Resident Viruses: The Resident virus implants itself in the memory of a computer. Basically, the original virus program is not required to infect new files or applications. Even when the original virus is deleted, the version stored in memory can be activated. This happens when the computer OS loads certain applications or functions. The resident viruses are troublesome due to the reason they can run unnoticed by antivirus and antimalware software by hiding in the system's RAM.

m. Rootkit Viruses: The rootkit virus is a malware type which secretly installs an illegal rootkit on an infected system. This opens the door for attackers and gives them full control of the system. The attacker will be able to fundamentally modify or disable functions and programs. Like other sophisticated viruses, the rootkit virus is also created to bypass antivirus software. The latest versions of major antivirus and antimalware programs include rootkit scanning.

n. System or Boot-record Infectors: The Boot-record Infectors infect executable code found in specific system areas on a disk. A s the name implies, they attach to the USB thumb drives and DOS boot sector on diskettes or the Master Boot Record on hard disks. Boot viruses are no more common these days as the latest devices rely less on physical storage media.

Virus preventions:

When our computers start slowing down or behaving in an unusual way, we are often quick to suspect that we have a virus. It might not be a virus, but it is likely that you have some sort of malware. Some are malicious, and others are just annoying. The worst culprits are the hijackers—malware programs that take over your browser, or worse yet, your computer. I have had to remove these types of evil programs from personal computers and work computers in the past, and I'm sure you have, too. Here are 10 tips on how to prevent malware from infecting your computer, keeping your hardware safe.

1. Install Anti-Virus/Malware Software: This tip may go without saying, and I almost just casually mentioned it in my opening paragraph. However, I have seen many computers—especially home computers—that don't have anti-virus/malware protection. This protection is a must-have first step in keeping your computer virus free.

2. Keep Your Anti-Virus Software Up to Date: Having protection software is the first step; maintaining it is the second. Free anti-virus software is better than nothing, but keep in mind that it's not the best solution. Microsoft does provide a security package for "free." It's free in that if you have Windows on your machine, you are

granted access, but you did pay for your Windows license. Many users aren't aware of this program, but it's actually decent protection.

3. Run Regularly Scheduled Scans with Your Anti-Virus Software: This too may seem like a no-brainer, but many of us forget to do this. Set up your software of choice to run at regular intervals. Once a week is preferred, but do not wait much longer between scans. It's difficult to work on your computer while your anti-virus software is running. One solution is to run the software at night when you aren't using your computer. However, we often turn off our computers at night, and so the scan never runs. Set your anti-virus software to run on a specific night, and always leave your computer running on that day. Make sure it doesn't shut off automatically or go into hibernation mode.

4. Keep Your Operating System Current: Whether you are running Windows, Mac OS X, Linux, or any other OS, keep it up to date. OS developers are always issuing security patches that fix and plug security leaks. These patches will help to keep your system secure. Similarly, keep your anti-virus software up to date. Viruses and malware are created all the time. Your scanning software is only as good as its database. It too must be as up to date as possible.

5. Secure Your Network: Many of our computers connect to our files, printers, or the Internet via a Wi-Fi connection. Make sure it requires a password to access it and that the password is strong. Never broadcast an open Wi-Fi connection. Use WPA or WPA2 encryption. WEP is no longer strong enough as it can be bypassed in

minutes by experts. It's also a great idea to not broadcast your SSID (the name of your Wi-Fi network). You can still access it with your device, you will just have to manually type in the SSID and the password. If you frequently have guests who use your Internet, provide a guest SSID that uses a different password, just in case your friends are evil hackers.

6. Think Before You Click: Avoid websites that provide pirated material. Do not open an email attachment from somebody or a company that you do not know. Do not click on a link in an unsolicited email. Always hover over a link (especially one with a URL shortener) before you click to see where the link is really taking you. If you have to download a file from the Internet, an email, an FTP site, a file-sharing service, etc., scan it before you run it. A good anti-virus software will do that automatically, but make sure it is being done.

7. Keep Your Personal Information Safe: This is likely the most difficult thing to do on the Internet. Many hackers will access your files not by brute force, but through social engineering. They will get enough of your information to gain access to your online accounts and will glean more of your personal data. They will continue from account to account until they have enough of your info that they can access your banking data or just steal your identity altogether. Be cautious on message boards and social media. Lock down all of your privacy settings, and avoid using your real name or identity on discussion boards.

8. Don't Use Open Wi-Fi: When you are at the local coffee shop, library, and especially the airport, don't use the

"free" open (non-password, non-encrypted) Wi-Fi. Think about it. If you can access it with no issues, what can a trained malicious individual do.

9. Use Multiple Strong Passwords: Never use the same password, especially on your bank account. Typically, we use the same email address or username for all of our accounts. Those are easy to see and steal. If you use the same password for everything, or on many things, and it is discovered, then it takes only seconds to hack your account. Use a strong password. Use lower case, upper case, numbers, and symbols in your password. Keep it easy to remember but difficult to guess. Do not use dates or pet names.

Mobile Internet:

Mobile Internet also known as mobile web, refers to browser-based Internet services accessed from handheld mobile devices, such as smartphones or feature phones, through a mobile or other wireless network.

GPS: GPS Stands for "Global Positioning System." GPS is a satellite navigation system used to determine the ground position of an object. GPS technology was first used by the United States military in the 1960s and expanded into civilian use over the next few decades. Today, GPS receivers are included in many commercial products, such as automobiles, smartphones, exercise watches, and GIS devices. The GPS system includes 24 satellites deployed in space about 12,000 miles (19,300 kilometers) above the earth's surface. They orbit the earth once every 12 hours at an extremely fast pace of roughly 7,000 miles per hour (11,200 kilometers per hour).

3G:

3G refers to the third generation of mobile telephony (that is, cellular) technology. The third generation, as the name suggests, follows two earlier generations. The first generation (1G) began in the early 80's with commercial deployment of Advanced Mobile Phone Service (AMPS) cellular networks. Early AMPS networks used Frequency Division Multiplexing Access (FDMA) to carry analog voice over channels in the 800 MHz frequency band.

The second generation (2G) emerged in the 90's when mobile operators deployed two competing digital voice standards. In North America, some operators adopted IS-95, which used Code Division Multiple Access (CDMA) to multiplex up to 64 calls per channel in the 800 MHz band. Across the world, many operators adopted the Global System for Mobile communication (GSM) standard, which used Time Division Multiple Access (TDMA) to multiplex up to 8 calls per channel in the 900 and 1800 MHz bands.

The International Telecommunications Union (ITU) defined the third generation (3G) of mobile telephony standards IMT-2000 to facilitate growth, increase bandwidth, and support more diverse applications. For example, GSM could deliver not only voice, but also circuit-switched data at speeds up to 14.4 Kbps. But to support mobile multimedia applications, 3G had to deliver packet-switched data with better spectral efficiency, at far greater speeds. However, to get from 2G to 3G, mobile operators had made "evolutionary" upgrades to existing networks while simultaneously planning their "revolutionary" new mobile broadband networks. This lead to the establishment of two distinct 3G families: 3GPP and 3GPP2.

4G:

Fourth generation wireless (4G) is an abbreviation for the fourth generation of cellular wireless standards and replaces the third generation of broadband mobile communications. The standards for 4G, set by the radio sector of the International Telecommunication Union (ITU-R), are denoted as International Mobile Telecommunications Advanced (IMT-Advanced). An IMT-Advanced cellular system is expected to securely provide mobile service users with bandwidth higher than 100 Mbps, enough to support high quality streaming multimedia content. Existing 3G technologies, often branded as Pre-4G (such as mobile WiMAX and 3G LTE), fall short of this bandwidth requirement. The majority of implementations branded as 4G do not comply with the full IMT-Advanced standard.

Wi-Fi:

Wi-Fi is a wireless networking technology that allows computers and other devices to communicate over a wireless signal. It describes network components that are based on one of the 802.11 standards developed by the IEEE and adopted by the Wi-Fi Alliance. Examples of Wi-Fi standards, in chronological order, include:

802.11a

802.11b

802.11g

802.11n

802.11ac

Wi-Fi is the standard way computers connect to wireless networks. Nearly all modern computers have built-in Wi-Fi chips that allows users to find and connect to wireless routers. Most mobile devices, video game systems, and other standalone devices also support Wi-Fi, enabling them to connect to wireless networks as well. When a device establishes a Wi-Fi connection with a router, it can communicate with the router and other devices on the network. However, the router must be connected to the Internet (via a DSL or cable modem) in order to provide Internet access to connected devices.

Bluetooth:

Bluetooth is a short-range wireless communication technology that allows devices such as mobile phones, computers, and peripherals to transmit data or voice wirelessly over a short distance. The purpose of Bluetooth is to replace the cables that normally connect devices, while still keeping the communications between them secure. The "Bluetooth" name is taken from a 10th-century Danish king named Harald Bluetooth, who was said to unite disparate, warring regional factions. Like its namesake, Bluetooth technology brings together a broad range of devices across many different industries through a unifying communication standard.

Social Network:

A social network is defined as a chain of individuals and their personal connections. Expanding one's connections with other people is a technique that can be used both for personal or business reasons. Social networking applications make use of the associations between individuals to further facilitate the creation of new connections with other people. This could be used to meet new friends and connect with old ones, as many people do on Facebook, Instagram, Twitter or to expand one's professional connections through a business network like LinkedIn.

Cloud Technology:

Cloud computing is the use of various services, such as software development platforms, servers, storage and software, over the internet, often referred to as the "cloud." In general, there are three cloud computing characteristics that are common among all cloud-computing vendors:

    a. The back-end of the application (especially hardware) is completely managed by a cloud vendor.
    b. A user only pays for services used (memory, processing time and bandwidth, etc.).
    c. Services are scalable.

Many cloud computing advancements are closely related to virtualization. The ability to pay on demand and scale quickly is largely a result of cloud computing vendors being able to pool resources that may be divided among multiple clients. It is common to categorize cloud computing services as infrastructure as a service (IaaS), platform as a service (PaaS) or software as a service (SaaS).

Virtual Lan Technology:

A VLAN is a custom network created from one or more existing LANs. It enables groups of devices from multiple networks (both wired and wireless) to be combined into a single logical network. The result is a virtual LAN that can be administered like a physical local area network. In order to create a virtual

LAN, the network equipment, such as routers and switches must support VLAN configuration. The hardware is typically configured using a software admin tool that allows the network administrator to customize the virtual network. The admin software can be used to assign individual ports or groups of ports on a switch to a specific VLAN.

Firewall:

A firewall is a network security system designed to prevent unauthorized access to or from a private network. Firewalls can be implemented as both hardware and software, or a combination of both. Network firewalls are frequently used to prevent unauthorized Internet users from accessing private networks connected to the Internet, especially intranets. All messages entering or leaving the intranet pass through the firewall, which examines each message and blocks those that do not meet the specified security criteria.

M-Commerce:

M-Commerce also called as Mobile Commerce involves the online transactions through the wireless handheld devices such as mobile phone, laptop, palmtop, tablet, or any other personal digital assistant. It does not require the user to sit at the computer that is plugged in and perform the commercial transactions. Through M-Commerce, people can perform several functions such as pay bills, buy and sell goods and services, access emails, book movie tickets, make railway reservations, order books, read and watch the news, etc.

Nanotechnology:

Nanotechnology is the study of phenomena and fine-tuning of materials at atomic, molecular and macromolecular scales, where properties differ significantly from those at a larger scale. Products based on nanotechnology are already in use and analysts expect markets to grow by hundreds of billions of euros during this decade. Or we can also define Nanotechnology is the understanding and control of matter at dimensions between approximately 1 and 100 nanometers, where unique phenomena enable novel applications. Encompassing nanoscale science, engineering, and technology, nanotechnology involves imaging, measuring, modeling, and manipulating matter at this length scale. Nanotechnology is an upcoming economic, business, and social phenomenon. Nano-advocates argue it will revolutionize the way we live, work and communicate.

Virtual Reality:

Virtual reality is an artificial environment that is created with software and presented to the user in such a way that the user suspends belief and accepts it as a real environment. On a computer, virtual reality is primarily experienced through two of the five senses: sight and sound. The simplest form of virtual reality is a 3-D image that can be explored interactively at a personal computer, usually by manipulating keys or the mouse so that the content of the image moves in some direction or zooms in or out. More sophisticated efforts involve such approaches as wrap-around display screens, actual rooms augmented with wearable computers, and haptics devices that let you feel the display images.

BPO:

BPO stands for Business Processing Outsourcing. BPO provides services like customer care, technical support through voice processes, tele-marketing, sales, etc. BPO requires Good communication skills and basic computer knowledge. A BPO is capable of handling both front end and back-end operations of an entity. BPO provides an array of services such as:

1. Customer care, i.e., call center, help desk, etc.
2. Human resources, i.e., recruitment and selection, training and placement, payroll processing, etc.
3. Technical support
4. Services related to finance and accounting.
5. Website services, i.e., web hosting, etc.
6. Transcription

KPO:

KPO stands for Knowledge Processing Outsourcing. KPO provides in-depth knowledge, expertise and analysis on complex areas like Legal Services, Business and Market Research, etc. KPO requires Specialized knowledge. The spectrum of services provided by KPO includes:

1. Investment research services
2. Market research services.
3. Data analytics.
4. Business research services
5. Others: Legal Process Outsourcing, Financial Process Outsourcing, Media Process Outsourcing.

YouTube:

YouTube is a video sharing service that allows users to watch videos posted by other users and upload videos of their own. The service was started as an independent website in 2005 and was acquired by Google in 2006. Videos that have been uploaded to YouTube may appear on the YouTube website and can also be posted on other websites, though the files are hosted on the YouTube server. The slogan of the YouTube website is

"Broadcast Yourself." This implies the YouTube service is designed primarily for ordinary people who want to publish videos they have created. While several companies and organizations also use YouTube to promote their business, the vast majority of YouTube videos are created and uploaded by amateurs.

Facebook:

Facebook is a popular free social networking website that allows registered users to create profiles, upload photos and video, send messages and keep in touch with friends, family and colleagues. The site, which is available in 37 different languages, includes public features such as:

1. Marketplace - allows members to post, read and respond to classified ads.
2. Groups - allows members who have common interests to find each other and interact.
3. Events - allows members to publicize an event, invite guests and track who plans to attend.
4. Pages - allows members to create and promote a public page built around a specific topic.
5. Presence technology - allows members to see which contacts are online and chat.

Within each member's personal profile, there are several key networking components. The most popular is arguably the Wall, which is essentially a virtual bulletin board. Messages left on a member's Wall can be text, video or photos. Another popular component is the virtual Photo Album. Photos can be uploaded from the desktop or directly from a smartphone camera. There is no limitation on quantity, but Facebook staff will remove inappropriate or copyrighted images. An interactive album feature allows the member's contacts (who are called generically called "friends") to comment on each other's photos and identify (tag) people in the photos. Another popular profile component is status updates, a microblogging feature that allows members to broadcast short Twitter-like announcements to their friends. All interactions are published in a news feed, which is distributed in real-time to the member's friends

LinkedIn:

LinkedIn is a social networking site designed specifically for the business community. The goal of the site is to allow registered members to establish and document networks of people they know and trust professionally. A LinkedIn member's profile page, which emphasizes skills, employment history and education, has professional network news feeds and a limited number of customizable modules. Basic membership for LinkedIn is free. Network members are called "connections." Unlike other free social networking sites like Facebook or Twitter, LinkedIn requires connections to have a pre-existing relationship. With basic membership, a member can only establish connections with someone he has worked with, knows professionally (online or offline) or has gone to school with. Connections up to three degrees away (see six degrees of separation) are seen as part of the member's network, but the member is not allowed to contact them through LinkedIn without an introduction. Premium subscriptions can be purchased to provide members with better access to contacts in the LinkedIn database. LinkedIn was co-founded by Reid Hoffman, a former Executive Vice President in charge of business and corporate development for PayPal. The site, which was launched in May 2003, currently has over 300 million members from 200 countries, representing 170 industries. According to Reid Hoffman, 27 percent of LinkedIn subscribers are recruiters. Microsoft acquired LinkedIn in June of 2016 for $26.2 billion.

Orkut:

Orkut is a social networking website developed and operated by Google Inc. Like other social networks, Orkut facilitates communication and interaction between friends, colleagues and family. Orkut users may upload videos and pictures and utilize a "like" feature to share interesting Web pages and content. The integrated GTalk, Google's instant messenger, enables users to chat directly from the Orkut page. Orkut is most popular with social networkers in Brazil, followed by India.

World Wide Web:

The World Wide Web (WWW) is combination of all resources and users on the Internet that are using the Hypertext Transfer Protocol (HTTP). "The World Wide Web is the universe of network-accessible information, an embodiment of human knowledge." The Web, as it's commonly known, is often confused with the internet. Although the two are intricately connected, they are different things. The internet is, as its name implies, a network -- a vast, global network that incorporates a multitude of lesser networks. As such, the internet consists of supporting infrastructure and other technologies. In contrast, the Web is a communications model that, through HTTP, enables the exchange of information over the internet.

Tim Berners-Lee is the inventor of the Web and the director of the W3C, the organization that oversees its development. Berners-Lee developed hypertext, the method of instant cross-referencing that supports communications on the Web, making it easy to link content on one web page to content located elsewhere. The introduction of hypertext revolutionized the way people used the internet. In 1989, Berners-Lee began work on the first World Wide Web server at CERN. He called the server "httpd" and dubbed the first client "WWW." Originally, WWW was just a WYSIWYG hypertext browser/editor that ran in the NeXTStep environment. The World Wide Web has been widely available since 1991.

Web browsers:

A web browser, or simply "browser," is an application used to access and view websites. Common web browsers include Microsoft Internet Explorer, Google Chrome, Mozilla Firefox, and Apple Safari. The primary function of a web browser is to render HTML, the code used to design or "mark up" webpages. Each time a browser loads a web page, it processes the HTML, which may include text, links, and references to images and other items, such as cascading style sheets and JavaScript functions. The browser processes these items, then renders them in the browser window.

Internet:

The Internet, sometimes called simply "the Net," is a worldwide system of computer networks - a network of networks in which users at any one computer can, if they have permission, get information from any other computer (and sometimes talk directly to users at other computers). It was conceived by the Advanced Research Projects Agency (ARPA) of the U.S.

government in 1969 and was first known as the ARPANet. The original aim was to create a network that would allow users of a research computer at one university to "talk to" research computers at other universities. A side benefit of ARPANet's design was that, because messages could be routed or rerouted in more than one direction, the network could continue to function even if parts of it were destroyed in the event of a military attack or other disaster.

Today, the Internet is a public, cooperative and self-sustaining facility accessible to hundreds of millions of people worldwide. Physically, the Internet uses a portion of the total resources of the currently existing public telecommunication networks. Technically, what distinguishes the Internet is its use of a set of protocols called UDP/IP (for Transmission Control Protocol/Internet Protocol). Two recent adaptations of Internet technology, the intranet and the extranet, also make use of the TCP/IP protocol. For most Internet users, electronic mail (email) practically replaced the postal service for short written transactions. People communicate over the Internet in a number of other ways including Internet Relay Chat (IRC), Internet telephony, instant messaging, video chat or social media.

History of Internet: The internet originated with the U.S. government, which began building a computer network in the 1960s known as ARPANET. In 1985, the U.S. National Science Foundation (NSF) commissioned the development of a university network backbone called NSFNET. The system was replaced by new networks operated by commercial internet service providers in 1995. The internet was brought to the public on a larger scale at around this time. Since then, the Internet has grown and evolved over time to facilitate services like:

- ❖ Email.
- ❖ Web-enabled audio/video conferencing services.
- ❖ Online movies and gaming.
- ❖ Data transfer/file-sharing, often through File Transfer Protocol (FTP).
- ❖ Instant messaging.
- ❖ Internet forums.
- ❖ Social networking.
- ❖ Online shopping.
- ❖ Financial services.

As a global network responsible for vast amounts of data transfer and process facilitation, the Internet is constantly evolving. For instance, an initial protocol called IPv4 distributing Internet Protocol (IP) addresses has largely been replaced by a new IPv6 model that will increase the number of addresses available for each continent around the globe. The Internet has also expanded beyond the traditional workstation, as the "Internet of Things," (IoT) as it's called, is born. There's still somewhat of a delineation between traditional Internet nodes, which use a classic web browser, and Internet-connected devices which will more commonly use reduced instruction set software, but the Internet of Things is blurring the line of where the Internet stops and the analog world begins.

In addition, there is a key framework that helps people to understand how the Internet is changing, and where it's likely to go in the future. This is composed of three versions or iterations of the World Wide Web, as defined above.

Web 1.0: is the original incarnation of the Internet as a place where most data was read-only. Web 1.0 is often described by experts as an Internet where the most common kinds of activity are passive – reading, doing research, or learning about products and services before making a purchase over traditional media, for example, by telephone.

Web 2.0: As engineers added things like JavaScript applets and modules to the web, Web 2.0 emerged. Web 2.0 is the read/write web or the functional web, where web fields and forms have allowed users to participate in transactions, upload resources or post their own suggestions in active conversation. Web 2.0 is, by most people's assertions, the Internet that we now use. The problem of "stateless" web-delivered functionality as is Web 2.0, is largely solved by digital "cookies," trackers that save individual user data in the browser to enable things like saved passwords. The trade-off is that user activity is inherently tracked: when a user erases the cookies, that session data is gone, and the user will have to start over as a new guest in any future sessions.

Web 3.0: is the posited future Internet called the "semantic web," where Internet data will have evolved relationships, and mapping will help automate a lot of what we now do on the Internet manually. The semantic web, proponents suggest, will be a web that is in many ways automated by linking individual virtual objects and websites together in a seamless manner. With that in mind, Web 3.0 may help us to do away with the current model of using cookies for session data retrieval. All of these changes show the general-purpose nature of the Internet and its broad scope in human societies. Defining groups like the Internet Engineering Task Force (IETF) and World Wide Web Consortium (W3C) continue to work on standards and universal approaches.

Features of Internet

The features are described below −

❖ Accessibility

An Internet is a global service and accessible to all. Today, people located in a remote part of an island or interior of Africa can also use Internet.

❖ Easy to Use

The software, which is used to access the Internet (web browser), is designed very simple; therefore, it can be easily learned and used. It is easy to develop.

❖ Interaction with Other Media

Internet service has a high degree of interaction with other media. For example, News and other magazine, publishing houses have extended their business with the help of Internet services.

❖ Low Cost

The development and maintenance cost of Internet service are comparatively low.

❖ Extension of Existing IT Technology

This facilitates the sharing of IT technology by multiple users in organizations and even facilitates other trading partners to use.

❖ Flexibility of Communication

Communication through Internet is flexible enough. It facilitates communication through text, voice, and video too. These services can be availed at both organizational and individual levels.

❖ Security

Last but not the least, Internet facility has to a certain extent helped the security system both at the individual and national level with components such as CCTV camera, etc.

❖ Internet Software

Internet Software comprises of all the tools needed for networking through computer. Following are a few important components of the Internet Software –

➢ Transmission Control Protocol/ Internet Protocol (TCP/IP)
➢ Dialer Software
➢ Interment Browser

Uses of the Internet

Some of the important usages of the internet are:

Online Businesses (E-commerce): Online shopping websites have made our life easier, e-commerce sites like Amazon, Flipkart, Myntra are providing very spectacular services with just one click and this is a great use of the Internet.

Cashless transactions: All the merchandising companies are offering services to their customers to pay the bills of the products online via various digital payment apps like Paytm, Google pay, etc. UPI payment gateway is also increasing day by day. Digital payment industries are growing at a rate of 50% every year too because of the INTERNET.

Education: It is the internet facility that provides a whole bunch of educational material to everyone through any server across the web. Those who are unable to attend physical classes can choose any course from the internet and can have the point-to-point knowledge of it just by sitting at home. High-class faculties are teaching online on digital platforms and providing quality education to students with the help of the Internet.

Social Networking: The purpose of social networking sites and apps is to connect people all over the world. With the help of social networking sites, we can talk, share videos, images with our loved ones when they are far away from us. Also, we can create groups for discussion or for meetings.

Entertainment: The Internet is also used for entertainment. There are numerous entertainment options available on the internet like watching movies, playing games, listening to music, etc. You can also download movies, games, songs, TV Serial, etc., easily from the internet.

Architecture of the Internet

The architecture of the Internet is ever-changing due to continuous changes in the technologies as well as the nature of the service provided. The heterogeneity and vastness of the Internet make it difficult to describe every aspect of its architecture.

The overall architecture can be described in three levels –

1. Backbone ISP (Internet Service Provider)

2. Regional ISPs

3. Clients

The following diagram shows the three levels –

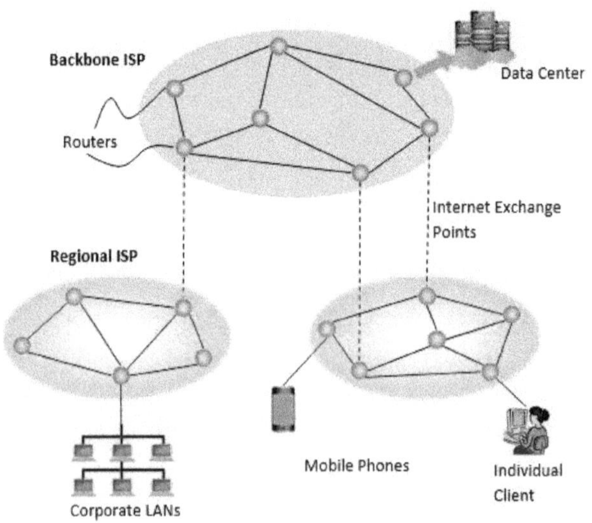

Backbone ISP (Internet Service Provider) – Backbone ISPs are large international backbone networks. They are equipped with thousands of routers and store enormous amounts of information in data centers, connected through high bandwidth fiber optic links. Everyone needs to connect with a backbone ISP to access the entire Internet.

There are different ways through which a client can connect to the ISP. A commonly used way is DSL (Digital Subscriber Line) which reuses the telephone connection of the user for transmission of digital data. The user uses a dial-up connection instead of the telephone call. Connectivity is also done by sending signals over cable TV system that reuses unused cable TV channels for data transmission. For high-speed Internet access, the connectivity can be done through FTTH (Fiber to the Home), that uses optical fibers for transmitting data. Nowadays, most Internet access is done through the wireless connection to mobile phones from fixed subscribers, who transmit data within their coverage area.

Internet addresses:

An Internet address uniquely identifies a node on the Internet. Internet address may also refer to the name or IP of a Web site (URL). The term Internet address can also represent someone's e-mail address.

An "IP," is a unique address that identifies a device on the Internet or a local network. It allows a system to be recognized by other systems connected via the Internet protocol.

There are two primary types of IP address formats used today — IPv4 and IPv6.

a. **IPv4:** An IPv4 address consist of four sets of numbers from 0 to 255, separated by three dots. For example, the IP address of TechTerms.com is 67.43.14.98. This number is used to identify the TechTerms website on the Internet. When you visit http://techterms.com in your web browser, the DNS system automatically translates the domain name "techterms.com" to the IP address "67.43.14.98."

There are three classes of IPv4 address sets that can be registered through the InterNIC. The smallest is Class C, which consists of 256 IP addresses (e.g. 123.123.123.xxx — where xxx is 0 to 255). The next largest is Class B, which contains 65,536 IP addresses (e.g. 123.123.xxx.xxx). The largest block is Class A, which contains 16,777,216 IP addresses (e.g. 123.xxx.xxx.xxx). The total number of IPv4 addresses ranges from 000.000.000.000 to 255.255.255.255. Because 256 = 28, there are 28 x 4 or 4,294,967,296 possible IP addresses. While this may seem like a large number, it is no longer enough to cover all the devices connected to the Internet around the world. Therefore, many devices now use IPv6 addresses.

b. **IPv6:** The IPv6 address format is much different than the IPv4 format. It contains eight sets of four hexadecimal digits and uses colons to separate each block. An example of an IPv6 address is: 2602:0445:0000:0000:a93e:5ca7:81e2:5f9d. There are 3.4 x 1038 or 340 undecillion) possible IPv6 addresses, meaning we shouldn't run out of IPv6 addresses anytime soon.

Internet Protocols

Internet Protocol (IP)

Internet Protocol is connectionless and unreliable protocol. It ensures no guarantee of successfully transmission of data. In order to make it reliable, it must be paired with reliable protocol such as TCP at the transport layer. Internet protocol transmits the data in form of a datagram as shown in the following diagram:

4	8	16	32 bits
VER	HLEN	D.S. type of service	Total length of 16 bits
Identification of 16 bits		Flags 3 bits	Fragmentation Offset (13 bits)
Time to live	Protocol	Header checksum (16 bits)	
Source IP address			
Destination IP address			
Option + Padding			

Points to remember:

- The length of datagram is variable.

- The Datagram is divided into two parts: header and data.

- The length of header is 20 to 60 bytes.

- The header contains information for routing and delivery of the packet.

Transmission Control Protocol (TCP)

TCP is a connection-oriented protocol and offers end-to-end packet delivery. It acts as back bone for connection. It exhibits the following key features:

- Transmission Control Protocol (TCP) corresponds to the Transport Layer of OSI Model.

- TCP is a reliable and connection-oriented protocol.

- TCP offers:

  - Stream Data Transfer.

  - Reliability.

  - Efficient Flow Control

  - Full-duplex operation.

  - Multiplexing.

- TCP offers connection oriented end-to-end packet delivery.

- TCP ensures reliability by sequencing bytes with a forwarding acknowledgement number that indicates to the destination the next byte the source expect to receive.

- It retransmits the bytes not acknowledged with in specified time period.

TCP Services

TCP offers following services to the processes at the application layer:

- Stream Delivery Service

- Sending and Receiving Buffers

- Bytes and Segments

- Full Duplex Service

- Connection Oriented Service

- Reliable Service

Stream Deliver Service

TCP protocol is stream oriented because it allows the sending process to send data as stream of bytes and the receiving process to obtain data as stream of bytes.

Sending and Receiving Buffers

It may not be possible for sending and receiving process to produce and obtain data at same speed, therefore, TCP needs buffers for storage at sending and receiving ends.

Bytes and Segments

The Transmission Control Protocol (TCP), at transport layer groups the bytes into a packet. This packet is called segment. Before transmission of these packets, these segments are encapsulated into an IP datagram.

Full Duplex Service

Transmitting the data in duplex mode means flow of data in both the directions at the same time.

Connection Oriented Service

TCP offers connection-oriented service in the following manner:

1. TCP of process-1 informs TCP of process – 2 and gets its approval.

2. TCP of process – 1 and TCP of process – 2 and exchange data in both the two directions.

3. After completing the data exchange, when buffers on both sides are empty, the two TCP's destroy their buffers.

User Datagram Protocol (UDP)

Like IP, UDP is connectionless and unreliable protocol. It doesn't require making a connection with the host to exchange data. Since UDP is unreliable protocol, there is no mechanism for ensuring that data sent is received.

UDP transmits the data in form of a datagram. The UDP datagram consists of five parts as shown in the following diagram:

Source Port	Destination Port
Length	UDP checksum
Data	

Points to remember:

- UDP is used by the application that typically transmit small amount of data at one time.

- UDP provides protocol port used i.e., UDP message contains both source and destination port number, that makes it possible for UDP software at the destination to deliver the message to correct application program.

File Transfer Protocol (FTP)

FTP is used to copy files from one host to another. FTP offers the mechanism for the same in following manner:

- FTP creates two processes such as Control Process and Data Transfer Process at both ends i.e. at client as well as at server.

- FTP establishes two different connections: one is for data transfer and other is for control information.

- Control connection is made between control processes while Data Connection is made between<="" b="" style="box-sizing: border-box;">

- FTP uses port 21 for the control connection and Port 20 for the data connection.

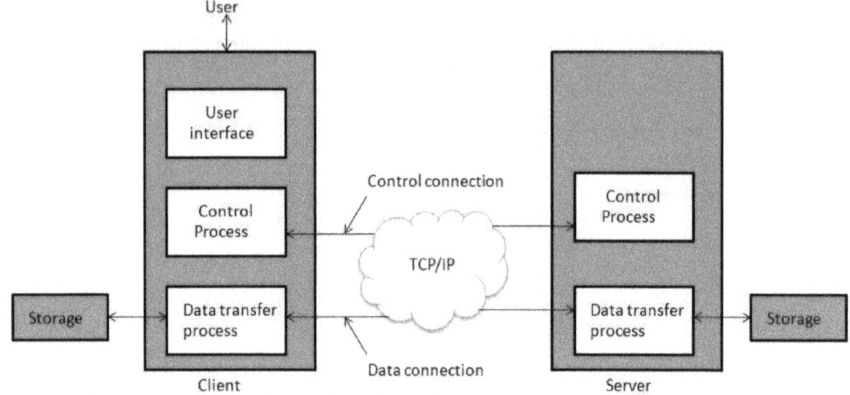

Trivial File Transfer Protocol (TFTP)

Trivial File Transfer Protocol is also used to transfer the files but it transfers the files without authentication. Unlike FTP, TFTP does not separate control and data information. Since there is no authentication exists, TFTP lacks in security features therefore it is not recommended to use TFTP.

Key points

- TFTP makes use of UDP for data transport. Each TFTP message is carried in separate UDP datagram.

- The first two bytes of a TFTP message specify the type of message.

- The TFTP session is initiated when a TFTP client sends a request to upload or download a file.

- The request is sent from an ephemeral UDP port to the UDP port 69 of an TFTP server.

Difference between FTP and TFTP

S.N.	Parameter	FTP	TFTP
1	Operation	Transferring Files	Transferring Files
2	Authentication	Yes	No
3	Protocol	TCP	UDP
4	Ports	21 – Control, 20 – Data	Port 3214, 69, 4012
5	Control and Data	Separated	Separated
6	Data Transfer	Reliable	Unreliable

Telnet

Telnet is a protocol used to log in to remote computer on the internet. There are a number of Telnet clients having user friendly user interface. The following diagram shows a person is logged in to computer A, and from there, he remotes logged into computer B.

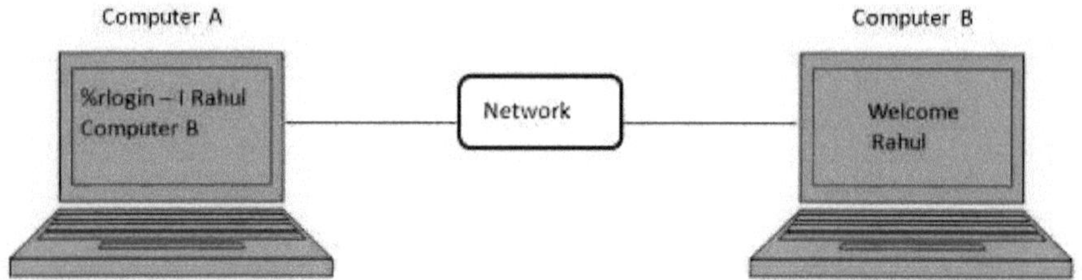

Hyper Text Transfer Protocol (HTTP)

HTTP is a communication protocol. It defines mechanism for communication between browser and the web server. It is also called request and response protocol because the communication between browser and server takes place in request and response pairs.

HTTP Request

HTTP request comprises of lines which contains:

- Request line

- Header Fields

- Message body

Key Points

- The first line i.e., the Request line specifies the request method i.e., Get or Post.

- The second line specifies the header which indicates the domain name of the server from where index.htm is retrieved.

HTTP Response

Like HTTP request, HTTP response also has certain structure. HTTP response contains:

- Status line

- Headers

- Message body

Introduction of internet of things

Internet of Things (IoT) is the networking of physical objects that contain electronics embedded within their architecture in order to communicate and sense interactions amongst each other or with respect to the external environment. In the upcoming years, IoT-based technology will offer advanced levels of services and practically change the way people lead their daily lives. Advancements in medicine, power, gene therapies, agriculture, smart cities, and smart homes are just a very few of the categorical examples where IoT is strongly established.

IoT is network of interconnected computing devices which are embedded in everyday objects, enabling them to send and receive data.

Over 9 billion 'Things' (physical objects) are currently connected to the Internet, as of now. In the near future, this number is expected to rise to a whopping 20 billion.

Main components used in IoT:
- Low-power embedded systems: Less battery consumption, high performance are the inverse factors that play a significant role during the design of electronic systems.

- Sensors: Sensors are the major part of any IoT applications. It is a physical device that measures and detect certain physical quantity and convert it into signal which can be provide as an input to processing or control unit for analysis purpose. Different types of Sensors :

1. Temperature Sensors

2. Image Sensors

3. Gyro Sensors

4. Obstacle Sensors

5. RF Sensor

6. IR Sensor

7. MQ-02/05 Gas Sensor

8. LDR Sensor

9. Ultrasonic Distance Sensor

- **Control Units:** It is a unit of small computer on a single integrated circuit containing microprocessor or processing core, memory and programmable input/output devices/peripherals. It is responsible for major processing work of IoT devices and all logical operations are carried out here.

- **Cloud computing:** Data collected through IoT devices is massive and this data has to be stored on a reliable storage server. This is where cloud computing comes into play. The data is processed and learned, giving more room for us to discover where things like electrical faults/errors are within the system.

- **Availability of big data:** We know that IoT relies heavily on sensors, especially in real-time. As these electronic devices spread throughout every field, their usage is going to trigger a massive flux of big data.

- **Networking connection:** In order to communicate, internet connectivity is a must where each physical object is represented by an IP address. However, there are only a limited number of addresses available according to the IP naming. Due to the growing number of devices, this naming system will not be feasible anymore. Therefore, researchers are looking for another alternative naming system to represent each physical object.

There are two ways of building IoT:

1. Form a separate internetwork including only physical objects.

2. Make the Internet ever more expansive, but this requires hard-core technologies such as rigorous cloud computing and rapid big data storage (expensive).

In the near future, IoT will become broader and more complex in terms of scope. It will change the world in terms of

"Anytime, anyplace, anything in connectivity."

IoT Enablers:

- **RFIDs:** uses radio waves in order to electronically track the tags attached to each physical object.

- **Sensors:** devices that are able to detect changes in an environment (ex: motion detectors).

- **Nanotechnology:** as the name suggests, these are extremely small devices with dimensions usually less than a hundred nanometers.

- **Smart networks:** (ex: mesh topology).

Working with IoT Devices:

- _**Collect and Transmit Data:**_ For this purpose, sensors are widely used they are used as per requirements in different application areas.

- _**Actuate device based on triggers produced by sensors or processing devices:**_ If certain condition is satisfied or according to user's requirements if certain trigger is activated then which action to performed that is shown by Actuator devices.

- _**Receive Information:**_ From network devices user or device can take certain information also for their analysis and processing purposes.

- _**Communication Assistance:**_ Communication assistance is the phenomena of communication between 2 network or communication between 2 or more IoT devices of same or different Networks. This can be achieved by different communication protocols like: MQTT, Constrained Application Protocol, ZigBee, FTP, HTTP etc.

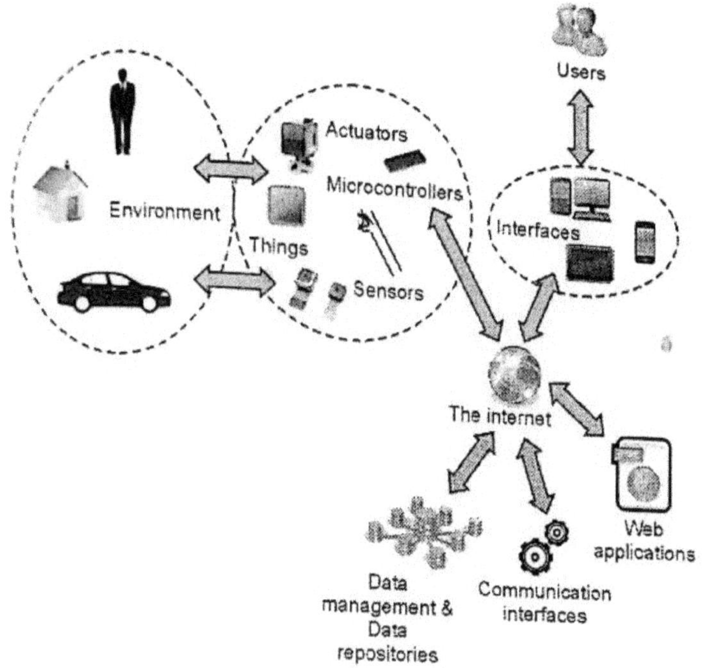

Working of IoT

Characteristics of IoT:

There are the following characteristics of IoT as follows. Let's discuss it one by one.

Connectivity: Connectivity is an important requirement of the IoT infrastructure. Things of IoT should be connected to the IoT infrastructure. Anyone, anywhere, anytime can connect, this should be guaranteed at all times. For example, connection between people through internet devices like mobile phones, and other gadgets, also connection between Internet devices such as routers, gateways, sensors, etc.

Intelligence and Identity– The extraction of knowledge from the generated data is very important. For example, a sensor generates data, but that data will only be useful if it is interpreted properly. Each IoT device has a unique identity. This identification is helpful in tracking the equipment and at times for querying its status.

Scalability – The number of elements connected to the IoT zone is increasing day by day. Hence, an IoT setup should be capable of handling the massive expansion. The data generated as an outcome is enormous, and it should be handled appropriately.

Dynamic and Self-Adapting (Complexity) – IoT devices should dynamically adapt themselves to the changing contexts and scenarios. Assume a camera meant for the surveillance. It should be adaptable to work in different conditions and different light situations (morning, afternoon,night).

Architecture – IoT architecture cannot be homogeneous in nature. It should be hybrid, supporting different manufacturers 'products to function in the IoT network. IoT is not owned by anyone engineering branch. IoT is a reality when multiple domains come together.

Safety – There is a danger of the sensitive personal details of the users getting compromised when all his/her devices are connected to the internet. This can cause a loss to the user.

Hence, data security is the major challenge. Besides, the equipment involved is huge. IoT networks may also be at the risk. Therefore, equipment safety is also critical.

Application Domains:

IoT is currently found in four different popular domains:

1) Manufacturing/Industrial business - 40.2%

2) Healthcare - 30.3%

3) Security - 7.7%

4) Retail - 8.3%

Modern Applications:

1. Smart Grids and energy saving
2. Smart cities
3. Smart homes/Home automation
4. Healthcare
5. Earthquake detection
6. Radiation detection/hazardous gas detection
7. Smartphone detection
8. Water flow monitoring
9. Traffic monitoring
10. Wearables
11. Smart door lock protection system

12. Robots and Drones

13. Healthcare and Hospitals, Telemedicine applications

14. Security

15. Biochip Transponders (For animals in farms)

Heart monitoring implants (Example Pacemaker, ECG real time tracking)

Intranet:

An intranet is a private network that is contained within an enterprise. It may consist of many interlinked local area networks and also use leased lines in the wide area network. Typically, an intranet includes connections through one or more gateway computers to the outside Internet. The main purpose of an intranet is to share company information and computing resources among employees. An intranet can also be used to facilitate working in groups and for teleconferences. An intranet uses TCP/IP, HTTP, and other Internet protocols and in general looks like a private version of the Internet. With tunneling, companies can send private messages through the public network, using the public network with special encryption/decryption and other security safeguards to connect one part of their intranet to another.

Typically, larger enterprises allow users within their intranet to access the public Internet through firewall servers that have the ability to screen messages in both directions so that company security is maintained. When part of an intranet is made accessible to customers, partners, suppliers, or others outside the company, that part becomes part of an extranet.

Domain names:

Domain names are used to identify one or more IP addresses. For example, the domain name microsoft.com represents about a dozen IP addresses. Domain names are used in URLs to identify particular Web pages. For example, in the URL http://www.pcwebopedia.com/index.html, the domain name is pcwebopedia.com. Every domain name has a suffix that indicates which top level domain (TLD) it belongs to. There are only a limited number of such domains. For example:

- gov - Government agencies
- edu - Educational institutions
- org - Organizations (nonprofit)
- mil – Military
- com - commercial business
- net - Network organizations
- ca – Canada
- th - Thailand

Because the Internet is based on IP addresses, not domain names, every Web server requires a Domain Name System (DNS) server to translate domain names into IP addresses.

Website

A website is a collection of many web pages, and web pages are digital files that are written using HTML (Hypertext Markup Language). To make your website available to every person in the world, it must be stored or hosted on a computer connected to the Internet round a clock. Such computers are known as a Web Server. The website's web pages are linked with hyperlinks and hypertext and share a common interface and design. The website might also contain some additional documents and files such as images, videos, or other digital assets.

With the Internet invading every sphere, we see websites for all kinds of causes and purposes. So, we can also say that a website can also be thought of as a digital environment capable of delivering information and solutions and promoting interaction between people, places, and things to support the goals of the organization it was created for.

Components of a Website: We know that a website is a collection of a webpages hosted on a web-server. These are the components for making a website.

➢ Webhost: Hosting is the location where the website is physically located. Group of webpages (linked webpages) licensed to be called a website only when the webpage is hosted on the webserver. The webserver is a set of files transmitted to user computers when they specify the website's address.
➢ Address: Address of a website also knows as the URL of a website. When a user wants to open a website then they need to put the address or URL of the website into the web browser, and the asked website is delivered by the webserver.
➢ Homepage: Home page is a very common and important part of a webpage. It is the first webpage that appears when a visitor visits the website. The home page of a website is very important as it sets the look and feel of the website and directs viewers to the rest of the pages on the website.

- ➤ Design: It is the final and overall look and feel of the website that has a result of proper use and integration elements like navigation menus, graphics, layout, navigation menus etc.
- ➤ Content: Every web page contained on the website together make up the content of the website. Good content on the webpages makes the website more effective and attractive.

The Navigation Structure: The navigation structure of a website is the order of the pages, the collection of what links to what. Usually, it is held together by at least one navigation menu.

Search engines:

search engine is software, typically accessed on the Internet, that searches a database of information according to the user's query. The engine provides a list of results that best match what the user is looking for. Today, there are many different search engines available on the Internet, each with their own abilities and features. The first search engine ever developed is considered Archie, which was used to search for FTP files and the first text-based search engine is considered Veronica. Today, the most popular and well-known search engine is Google. Other popular search engines include AOL, Ask.com, Baidu, Bing, and Yahoo.

Electronic mail:

Electronic mail (E-mail) is the exchange of computer-stored messages by telecommunication. (Some publications spell it email; we prefer the currently more established spelling of e-mail.) E-mail messages are usually encoded in ASCII text.

However, you can also send non-text files, such as graphic images and sound files, as attachments sent in binary streams. E-mail was one of the first uses of the Internet and is still the most popular use. A large percentage of the total traffic over the Internet is e-mail. E-mail can also be exchanged between online service provider users and in networks other than the Internet, both public and private.

E-mail can be distributed to lists of people as well as to individuals. A shared distribution list can be managed by using an e-mail reflector. Some mailing lists allow you to subscribe by sending a request to the mailing list administrator. A mailing list that is administered automatically is called a list server.

Voice mail:

Voicemail is a method of storing voice messages electronically for later retrieval by intended recipients. Callers leave short messages that are stored on digital media (or, in some older systems, on analog recording tape). Originally, voicemail was developed for telephony as a means to prevent missed calls, and also to facilitate call screening. In recent years, voicemail has become integrated with the Internet, allowing users to receive incoming messages on traditional computers as well as on tablets and mobile phones. Microsoft Exchange is a popular platform for voicemail with desktop and notebook computers. Users can play their voicemail messages either as audio (MP3) or as text. In order to play a voicemail or read it as text, the user simply clicks on an inbox item, just as would be done with an ordinary e-mail message. One particularly interesting development is the integration of voicemail with e-mail. Google Voice.

Cloud computing:

In simple terms, cloud computing is a range of services delivered over the internet, or "the cloud." It means using remote servers to store and access data instead of relying on local hard drives and private datacenters.

Before cloud computing existed, organizations had to purchase and maintain their own servers to meet business needs. This required buying enough server space to reduce the risk of downtime and outages, and to accommodate peak traffic volume. As a result, large amounts of server space went unused for much of the time. Today's cloud service providers allow companies to reduce the need for onsite servers, maintenance personnel, and other costly IT resources.

There are three types of cloud computing deployment models: private cloud, public cloud, and hybrid cloud.

Private cloud: provides a proprietary cloud environment dedicated to a single business entity, with physical components stored on-premises or at a vendor's datacenter. Because the private cloud is only accessible to a single business, this model offers a high degree of control. Advantages include customized architecture, advanced security protocols, and the ability to extend computing resources in a virtualized environment as needed. In many cases, an organization maintains a private cloud infrastructure on-site while delivering cloud computing services to internal users via the intranet. In other instances, the organization contracts with a third-party cloud vendor to host and maintain exclusive servers off site.

Public cloud: uses the internet to store and manage access to data and applications. It's completely virtualized, providing an environment where shared resources are leveraged as needed. Because these resources are delivered over the web, the public cloud deployment model allows organizations to scale more easily — the ability to pay for cloud resources as needed is a huge advantage over local servers. In addition, public cloud service providers offer robust security measures to protect user data from being accessed by other tenants.

Hybrid cloud: combines private and public cloud models, allowing organizations to leverage the benefits of shared resources while using existing IT infrastructure for critical security requirements. The hybrid cloud model allows companies to store confidential data internally and access it via applications running in the public cloud. To comply with privacy regulations, for example, an organization could store sensitive user data in a private cloud and perform resource-intensive computation in the public cloud.

In addition, businesses can choose to take a multi-cloud approach, which means they use more than one public cloud service. This approach can be used to distribute workloads across multiple cloud platforms, allowing organizations to optimize their environments for performance, flexibility, and cost savings.

Software as a Service (SaaS)

Traditionally, software was installed directly on each individual device. With the software as a service (SaaS) computing model, web applications are hosted in the cloud to reduce costs through pay-as-you-go pricing. End users can easily connect to the cloud application through a web browser or mobile device, and there's no need for IT departments to get involved with management or maintenance. Examples include Gmail, Salesforce CRM, and Right Signature, as well as cloud storage services like OneDrive and Dropbox.

Infrastructure as a Service (IaaS)

The infrastructure as a service (IaaS) computing model moves an organization's entire datacenter to the cloud. The business rents virtual machines (VMs), virtual servers, operating systems, and other IT infrastructure on a pay-as-you-go basis. The cloud service provider is responsible for maintaining all data storage servers and networking hardware, eliminating the need for a resource-intensive, on-site installation. Examples include Microsoft Azure, Google Cloud, Oracle Cloud, and Amazon Web Services (AWS).

Platform as a Service (PaaS)

The platform as a service computing model gives organizations the power to develop software without needing to maintain the backend environment. PaaS vendors optimize environments for each tenant's unique needs, and often include supplemental development tools such as storage resources, compile services, and version control.

Chapter 5: Number System and Data Information Concepts

Introduction to number system:

There are four types of number system

1. **Decimal:** It has a base 10 and uses ten digits or symbols 0, 1, 2, 3, 4, 5, 6, 7, 8, 9.
2. **Binary:** It has a base of 2 i.e., it uses only two different symbols 0 and 1.
3. **Octal:** It has a base of 8i.e., it uses eight different symbols 0,1,2,3,4,5,6,7.
4. **Hexadecimal:** It has a base of 16i.e., it uses 16 different symbols 0,1,2,3,4,5,6,7,8,9, A, B, C, D, E, F.

Decimal number system:

It is defined as the number of different digits which can occur in each position in the number system. A decimal system uses a base of 10, meaning that it contains ten unique symbols (or digits) namely 0, 1, 2, 3, 4, 5, 6, 7, 8, 9. Examples are 100_{10}, 240_{10} and 24_{10}.

The absolute value of each digit is fixed but its position is determined by its position in overall number. For example, the position value of 5 in 5555 is quite different as shown in fig. below:

So, $5555 = 5 \times 10^3 + 5 \times 10^2 + 5 \times 10^1 + 5 \times 10^0$

Similarly, the number 1245 may be expressed as

$1245 = 1 \times 10^3 + 2 \times 10^2 + 4 \times 10^1 + 5 \times 10^0$

It is to be noted that the number 5 (last number) is the least significant digit (LSD) while the number 1 (first number) is the most significant digit (MSD).

Again, the number 42561.893 can be written as

$42561.893 = 4 \times 10^4 + 2 \times 10^3 + 5 \times 10^2 + 6 \times 10^1 + 1 \times 10^0 + 8 \times 10^{-1} + 9 \times 10^{-2} + 3 \times 10^{-3}$

It is seen that the position values are found by raising the base of the number system to the power of position, also powers are numbered to the left of decimal point starting with 0 and to the right of the decimal point starting with -1.

Binary number system:

Like decimal system it has base and also the same type of position value system. Any binary number is called bit. It has base 2, since it can use only two digits 0 and 1. All binary numbers consists of string of 0s and 1s. Examples are 101_{10}, 111_{10} and 10_{10} which are read as one-zero-one, one-one-one and one-zero to avoid confusion with decimal numbers. In binary system the position value of each bit corresponds to some power of two. In binary system binary point corresponds to decimal point in decimal system. Therefore, the value of each binary number increases in power of 2 starting with 0 to the left of the binary point and decreases to the right of the binary point starting with power -1. The position value of each bit along with a 6-bit binary number 101.010 is shown below

MSD			Binary point			LSD
1	0	1	.	0	1	0
2^2	2^1	2^0		2^{-1}	2^{-2}	2^{-3}

In binary number the extreme left bit carries maximum weight and is called most significant digit (MSD), Whereas the extreme right digit has least weight and is called least significant digit (LSD).

Octal number system:

The octal number system has eight basic symbols or digits. The digits are 0, 1, 2, 3, 4, 5, 6, 7. (There is no 8 or 9). These digits have exactly same physical meaning as in decimal system. So, it has base 8, examples are $(164)_8$, $(247)_8$ etc.

For counting beyond 7, two-digit combinations are formed taking the second digit followed by the first, then second followed by second, then second by third and so on. That is after 7 the next successive numbers are 10, 11, 12, 13.14…….

The position value of different digits is given by different powers of 8 as shown below

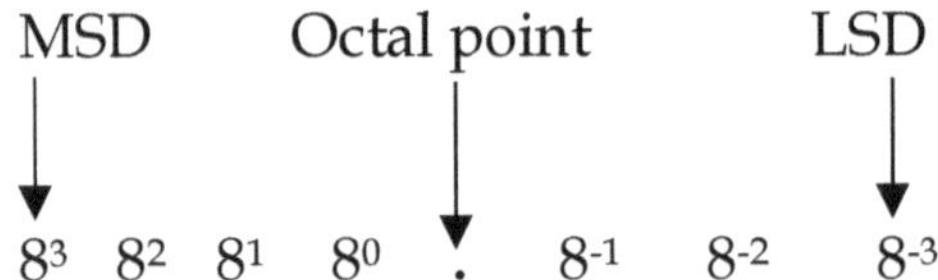

The digits on left hand side is most significant digit (MSD), Whereas on right hand side is least significant digit (LSD).

For example, the decimal equivalent of octal 247 is

$$2 \quad 4 \quad 7$$

Position value 8^2 8^1 8^0

Therefore, Decimal equivalent is $2\times8^2 + 4\times8^1 + 7\times8^0 = (167)_{10}$.

Hexadecimal number system:

This number system was investigated to express binary numbers concisely and is used for memorizing the different numbers in computer. It has base of 16 and uses sixteen distinct counting digits 0 to 15 of decimal system. The numbers beyond 9 are expressed by A, B, C, D, E, F. Hence the digits of hexadecimal system are

0, 1, 2, 3, 4, 5, 6, 7, 8, 9, A, B, C, D, E, F.

The position value of each digit is in ascending powers of 16 for integers and descending powers of 16 for fractions. The counting beyond F in hexadecimal number system is done by two-digit combination. The counting after F is done by taking second digit followed by first, the second digit by second, then second followed by third and so on.

The following table represents the numbers of all four number systems up to 20.

Decimal	Binary	Octal	Hexadecimal
0	0	0	0
1	1	1	1
2	10	2	2
3	11	3	3
4	100	4	4
5	101	5	5
6	110	6	6
7	111	7	7

8	1000	10	8
9	1001	11	9
10	1010	12	A
11	1011	13	B
12	1100	14	C
13	1101	15	D
14	1110	16	E
15	1111	17	F
16	10000	20	10
17	10001	21	11
18	10010	22	12
19	10011	23	13
20	10100	24	14

Conversion from one number system to another: Binary Number System to Another

i)   **Binary to decimal conversion: -**

In this method, each binary digit of the number is multiplied by its positional weight and the product terms are added to obtain decimal number.

For example:

a. Convert $(10101)_2$ to decimal.
   Sol:

(Positional weight) $2^4\ 2^3\ 2^2\ 2^1\ 2^0$

Binary number   10101

$= (1 \times 2^4) + (0 \times 2^3) + (1 \times 2^2) + (0 \times 2^1) + (1 \times 2^0)$

$$= (16 + 0 + 4 + 0 + 1)$$
$$= (21)_{10}$$

b. Convert $(111.101)_2$ to decimal.

Sol:

$(111.101)_2 = (1 \times 2^2) + (1 \times 2^1) + (1 \times 2^0) + (1 \times 2^{-1}) + (0 \times 2^{-2}) + (1 \times 2^{-3})$

$$= 4 + 2 + 1 + 0.5 + 0 + 0.125$$
$$= (7.625)_{10}$$

ii) **Binary to Octal conversion**: -

For conversion binary to octal the binary numbers are divided into groups of 3 bits each, starting at the binary point and proceeding towards left and right.

Octal	Binary	Octal	Binary
0	000	4	100
1	001	5	101
2	010	6	110
3	011	7	111

For example:

a. Convert $(101111010110.110110011)_2$ into octal.

Group of 3 bits are   101 111 010 110 . 110   110011

Convert each group into octal =   5   7   2 6 . 6   6   3

The result is

$(5726.663)_8$

(ii) Convert $(10101111001.0111)_2$ into octal.

Sol :

Binary number   10   101   111 001 . 011   1

Group of 3 bits are = 010   101   111 001 . 011   100

Convert each group into octal =   2   5   7   1 .   3   4

The result is $(2571.34)_8$

iii) Binary to Hexadecimal conversion: -

For conversion binary to hexadecimal number the binary numbers starting from the binary point, groups are made of 4 bits each, on either side of the binary point.

For example:

a. Convert $(1011011011)_2$ into hexadecimal.

Sol: Given Binary number   10   1101   1011

Group of 4 bits are   0010   1101   1011

Convert each group into hex =2   D   B

The result is $(2DB)_{16}$

b. Convert $(01011111011.011111)_2$ into hexadecimal.

Sol: Given Binary number

010   1111   1011   .   0111   11

Group of 4 bits are

0010   1111   1011   .   0111   1100

Convert each group into octal

<table>
<tr><td>2</td><td>F</td><td>B</td><td>.</td><td>7</td><td>C</td></tr>
</table>

The result is $(2FB.7C)_{16}$

Decimal Number System to Another: -

(a) Decimal to binary conversion: -

In the conversion the integer number are converted to the desired base using successive division by the base or radix.

For example:

(i) Convert $(52)_{10}$ into binary.

Solution:

Divide the given decimal number successively by 2 read the integer part remainder upwards to get equivalent binary number. Multiply the fraction part by 2. Keep the integer in the product as it is and multiply the new fraction in the product by 2. The process is continued and the integer are read in the products from top to bottom.

2	52	
2	26	0
2	13	0
2	6	1
2	3	0
2	1	1
	0	0

Result of $(52)10$ is $(110100)2$

(II)　　Convert $(105.15)10$ into binary.

Solution:

Integer Part

2	105	
2	52	1
2	26	0
2	13	0
2	6	1
2	3	0
2	1	1
2	0	1

Fraction

$0.15 \times 2 = 0.30$

$0.30 \times 2 = 0.60$

$0.60 \times 2 = 1.20$

$0.20 \times 2 = 0.40$

$0.40 \times 2 = 0.80$

$0.80 \times 2 = 1.60$

Result of $(105.15)_{10}$ is $(1101001.001001)_2$

(b)Decimal to octal conversion: -

To convert the given decimal integer number to octal, successively divide the given number by 8 till the quotient is 0. To convert the given decimal fractions to octal successively multiply the decimal fraction and the subsequent decimal fractions by 8 till the product is 0 or till the required accuracy is obtained.

For example:

(i) Convert $(378.93)_{10}$ into octal.

Solution:

8	378	
8	47	2
8	5	7
8	0	5

$0.93 \times 8 = 7.44$

$0.44 \times 8 = 3.52$

$0.52 \times 8 = 4.16$

$0.16 \times 8 = 1.28$

Result of $(378.93)_{10}$ is $(572.7341)_8$

(c)Decimal to hexadecimal conversion: -

The decimal to hexadecimal conversion is same as octal.

For example:

(i) Convert $(2598.675)_{10}$ into hexadecimal.

Solution:

	Decimal	Reminder	Hexa
16	2598		
16	162	6	6
16	10	2	2
	0	10	A

	Hexa
0.93 x 8 = 7.44	A
0.44 x 8 = 3.52	C
0.52 x 8 = 4.16	C
0.16 x 8 = 1.28	C

Result of $(2598.675)_{10}$ is $(A26.ACCC)_{16}$

Octal Number System to Another

i. **Octal to binary conversion:** -To convert a given an octal number to binary, replace each octal digit by its 3- bit binary equivalent.

For example:

Convert $(367.52)_8$ into binary.

Solution:

Given Octal number is   3   6   7 .   5   2

Convert each group octal   = 011   110   111 .   101   010

to binary

Result of $(367.52)_8$ is $(011110111.101010)_2$

ii.   Octal to decimal conversion: -

For conversion octal to decimal number, multiply each digit in the octal number by the weight of its position and add all the product terms

For example: -

Convert $(4057.06)_8$ to decimal

Solution:

$(4057.06)_8$ = $4 \times 8^3 + 0 \times 8^2 + 5 \times 8^1 + 7 \times 8^0 + 0 \times 8^{-1} + 6 \times 8^{-2}$

$\qquad\qquad = 2048 + 0 + 40 + 7 + 0 + 0.0937$

$\qquad\qquad = (2095.0937)_{10}$

Result is $(2095.0937)_{10}$

iii.   Octal to hexadecimal conversion: -

For conversion of octal to Hexadecimal, first convert the given octal number to binary and then binary number to hexadecimal.

For example: -

Convert $(756.603)_8$ to hexadecimal.

Solution: -

Given octal no.　　　　7　　5　　6　. 6　0　3

Convert each octal digit to binary

　　　　　=　　111　101　　110　. 110　000　011

Group of 4bits are　=　　0001 1110　1110　. 1100 0001 1000

Convert 4 bits group to hex.

　　　　　=　　1　　E　　E　. C　1　8

Result is $(1EE.C18)_{16}$

Hexadecimal Number System

i.　**<u>Hexadecimal to binary conversion: -</u>**

For conversion of hexadecimal to binary, replace hexadecimal digit by its 4-bit binary group.

For example:

Convert $(3A9E.B0D)_{16}$ into binary.

Solution:

Given Hexadecimal number is

　　　　　3　　A　9　　E　. B　0　　D

Convert each hexadecimal digit to 4 bit binary

　　　　= 0011　　1010　1001　1110 .　10110000 1101

Result of $(3A9E.B0D)_8$ is $(0011101010011110.101100001101)_2$

ii.   <u>**Hexadecimal to decimal conversion: -**</u>

For conversion of hexadecimal to decimal, multiply each digit in the hexadecimal number by its position weight and add all those product terms.

For example: -

Convert $(A0F9.0EB)_{16}$ to decimal

Solution:

$(A0F9.0EB)_{16}$ $=$ $(10 \times 16^3) + (0 \times 16^2) + (15 \times 16^1) + (9 \times 16^0)$
$+ (0 \times 16^{-1}) + (14 \times 16^{-2}) + (11 \times 16^{-3})$

$$= \quad 40960 + 0 + 240 + 9 + 0 + 0.0546 + 0.0026$$
$$= \quad (41209.0572)_{10}$$

Result is $(41209.0572)_{10}$

iii.   <u>**Hexadecimal to Octal conversion: -**</u>

For conversion of hexadecimal to octal, first convert the given hexadecimal number to binary and then binary number to octal.

For example: -

Convert $(B9F.AE)_{16}$ to octal.

Solution :-

Given hexadecimal no.is   B 9   F . A   E

Convert each hex. digit to binary

$$= \quad 1011 \quad 1001 \quad 1111 . \quad 1010 \, 1110$$

Group of 3 bits are $=$ 101 110 011 111 . 101 011 100

Convert 3 bits group to octal.

$$= \quad 5 \quad 6 \quad 3 \; 7 \quad . \; 5 \quad 3 \quad 4$$

Result is $(5637.534)_8$.

Representation of Characters:

- Everything represented by a computer is represented by binary sequences.

- A common non-integer needed to be represented is characters.

- We use standard encodings (binary sequences) to represent characters.

A standard code ASCII (American Standard for Computer Information Interchange) defines what character is represented by each sequence. Characters must somehow be represented in the computer using the 1's and 0's that the hardware works with. How they are represented is arbitrary, but to make sure that characters used on one computer are understood correctly by another, there are standards defined. The most common standard is called ASCII (American Standard Code for Information Interchange). In ASCII, there are 128 characters to be represented, so each character is stored in one byte. Here is one representation of the ASCII character set We can divide the character set into different classes:

- Alphabetic characters including: o lower case letters - 'a'..'z' o upper case letters - 'A'..'Z'

• Digit characters - '0'..'9' • Punctuation characters - '.',';',',', etc.

• White space characters - ' ','\n','\t', etc.

• Special characters - '@',' < ', ' >', etc.

• Control characters - '^A','^B', etc.

Each character has a numeric representation. How can we find that out? printf("The numeric representation of %c is %d\n",'a','a'); The characters whose ASCII values are between 32 and 126 are said to be printable characters. The others have special meanings, for example, '^J' is the newline ('\n') character in Unix, '^I' is the tab ('\t') character.

Examples: 0100 0001 is 41 (hex) or 65 (decimal). It represents `A'

0100 0010 is 42 (hex) or 66 (decimal). It represents `B'

Different bit patterns are used for each different character that needs to be represented. The code has some nice properties. If the bit patterns are compared, (pretending they represent integers), then `A' < `B'

This is good, because it helps with sorting things into alphabetical order.

Notes: `a' (61 hex) is different than `A' (41 hex) `8' (38 hex) is different than the integer 8

the digits: `0' is 48 (decimal) or 30 (hex)

`9' is 57 (decimal) or 39 (hex)

Because of this, code must deal with both characters and integers correctly.

Representation of Integers:

Integers are whole numbers or fixed-point numbers with the radix point fixed after the least-significant bit. They are contrast to real numbers or floating-point numbers, where the position of the radix point varies. It is important to take note that integers and floating-point numbers are treated differently in computers. They have different representation and are processed differently (e.g., floating-point numbers are processed in a so-called floating-point processor). Computers use a fixed number of bits to represent an integer. The commonly-used bit-lengths for integers are 8-bit, 16-bit, 32-bit or 64-bit. The term integer is used in computer engineering/science to refer to a data type which represents some finite subset of the mathematical integers. Integers may be unsigned or signed. Common integer data types and ranges.

Bits	Name
8	Byte, Octal
16	Half word, Word
32	Word, Double word, Long word
64	Double word, longword, long long, quad, quadword
128	Octal word
n	n-bit integer (general case)

1. Unsigned Integers: can represent zero and positive integers.

2. Signed Integers: can represent zero, positive and negative integers. Three representation schemes had been proposed for signed integers:

a. Sign-Magnitude representation

b. 1's Complement representation

c. 2's Complement representation

You, as the programmer, need to decide on the bit-length and representation scheme for your integers, depending on your application's requirements. Suppose that you need a counter for counting a small quantity from 0 up to 200, you might choose the 8-bit unsigned integer scheme as there is no negative numbers involved.

i) n-bit Unsigned Integers: Unsigned integers can represent zero and positive integers, but not negative integers. The value of an unsigned integer is interpreted as "the magnitude of its underlying binary pattern". Example 1: Suppose that n=8and the binary pattern is 0100 0001B, the value of this unsigned integer is $1×2^0 + 1×2^6 = 65D$.   Example 2: Suppose that n=16and the binary pattern is 0001 0000 0000 1000B, the value of this unsigned integer is $1×2^3 + 1×2^{12} = 4104D$.

An n-bit pattern can represent 2^n distinct integers. An n-bit unsigned integer can represent integers from 0 to $(2^n)-1$, as tabulated below:

ii) Signed Integers: Signed integers can represent zero, positive integers, as well as negative integers. Three representation schemes are available for signed integers:

1. Sign-Magnitude representation

2. 1's Complement representation

3. 2's Complement representation

In all the above three schemes, the most-significant bit (msb) is called the sign bit. The sign bit is used to represent the sign of the integer - with 0 for positive integers and 1 for negative integers. The magnitude of the integer, however, is interpreted differently in different schemes.

iii) n-bit Sign Integers in Sign-Magnitude Representation: In sign-magnitude representation:

• The most-significant bit (msb) is the sign bit, with value of 0 representing positive integer and 1 representing negative integer.

• The remaining n-1 bits represents the magnitude (absolute value) of the integer. The absolute value of the integer is interpreted as "the magnitude of the (n-1)-bit binary pattern". **Example 1:**

Suppose that n=8 and the binary representation is 0 100 0001B.

Sign bit is 0 ⇒

positive Absolute value is 100 0001B = 65D

Hence, the integer is +65D

The drawbacks of sign-magnitude representation are:

1. There are two representations (0000 0000B and 1000 0000B) for the number zero, which could lead to inefficiency and confusion.

2. Positive and negative integers need to be processed separately.

iv) Computers use 2's Complement Representation for Signed Integers

We have discussed three representations for signed integers: signed-magnitude, 1's complement and 2's complement. Computers use 2's complement in representing signed integers. This is because:

1. There is only one representation for the number zero in 2's complement, instead of two representations in sign-magnitude and 1's complement.

2. Positive and negative integers can be treated together in addition and subtraction. Subtraction can be carried out using the "addition logic".

REPRESENTATION OF FRACTIONS:

Use a "binary point" to separate positive from negative powers of two -- just like "decimal point."! 2's comp addition and subtraction still work • only if binary points are aligned 00101000.101!"#$%&' (+ 11111110.110!) *$&' (00100111.011! +, $+- (Thus, you can pick some part of a 32-bit computer word and decide where the binary point should be. Let's say we pick the middle of the word somewhere. This gives 1 bit of sign, 15 bits of integer, and 16 bits of fraction. Thus, one can have numbers from about - 32,767 to +32,767 with about 4½ decimal digits of fractional precision.

If you use this technique, you must convert numbers from the bit representation to decimal representation correctly. Pascal and C do not provide this flexibility in conversion, but some other programming languages do. PL/I for example allows you to declare numeric variables with the number of bits and where the binary point should be located. PL/I then build code to do the shifting and adjusting for you, and its input/output routines also work properly. However, one can always write conversion subroutines in other languages that do work properly so that you can both input fractional quantities and output them properly.

Note that the rules for binary arithmetic on these fractional numbers are the same as it is for integers, so it requires no change in the hardware to deal with binary fractions. That is this fractional representation is isomorphic to the binary twos-complement integer representation that the machine uses. It only requires that you think the numbers are fractions and that you understand and treat properly the binary-point (the binary equivalent of the decimal point). For example, you can only meaningfully add two numbers if the binary point is aligned. Of course, the computer will add them no matter where you think the binary point is. This is just like decimal arithmetic where you must add two numbers with the decimal points aligned if you want the right answer.

One can shift the binary point of a number by multiplying or dividing by the proper power of two, just as one shifts the decimal point by multiplying or dividing by a power of ten. Most machines also provide arithmetic shift operations that shift the bit representation of the number right or left more quickly than a multiply instruction would. An arithmetic right shift of 3 is a binary division by 2 3 or 8; a left shift is a binary multiplication. Arithmetic right shifts usually copy the sign bit so that negative numbers stay negative. Arithmetic left shifts introduce zeros from the right side of the number. If the sign bit changes in an arithmetic left shift, then the number has overflowed.

One is not restricted to scaling in the binary representation, one can also scale in the decimal representation. The rules for decimal scaling are the same as in the table above. For example, if you read in an integer but you know that it contains a number with two `implied' decimal digits, i.e. the number 500 represents 5 with a q=2. You treat it that way in the machine, multiply it by 2.1 (21 with a q=1), the result is (10500, with q=3). Now you can correctly output the result with the decimal point properly placed because you know the q=3, 10.500. Again, you must be careful to only add and subtract numbers with the same decimal scale, and carefully scale the numbers around multiplication and division to preserve both the high-order digits while maintaining the required precision after the decimal point.

Binary Arithmetic:

Binary arithmetic is essential part of all the digital computers and many other digital systems.

Binary Addition

It is a key for binary subtraction, multiplication, division. There are four rules of binary addition.

Case	A	+	B	Sum	Carry
1	0	+	0	0	0
2	0	+	1	1	0
3	1	+	0	1	0
4	1	+	1	0	1

In fourth case, a binary addition is creating a sum of (1 + 1 = 10) i.e., 0 is written in the given column and a carry of 1 over to the next column.

Example – Addition

0011010 + 001100 = 00100110		
	1 1	carry
	0 0 1 1 0 1 0	$= 26_{10}$
	+ 0 0 0 1 1 0 0	$= 12_{10}$
	0 1 0 0 1 1 0	$= 38_{10}$

Binary Subtraction

Subtraction and borrow, these two words will be used very frequently for the binary subtraction. There are four rules of binary subtraction.

Case	A - B	Subtract	Borrow
1	0 - 0	0	0
2	1 - 0	1	0
3	1 - 1	0	0
4	0 - 1	0	1

Example – Subtraction

0011010 - 001100 = 00001110		
	1 1	borrow
	0 0 1 1 0 1 0	$= 26_{10}$
	- 0 0 0 1 1 0 0	$= 12_{10}$
	0 0 0 1 1 1 0	$= 14_{10}$

Binary Multiplication

Binary multiplication is similar to decimal multiplication. It is simpler than decimal multiplication because only 0s and 1s are involved. There are four rules of binary multiplication.

Case	A	x	B	Multiplication
1	0	x	0	0
2	0	x	1	0
3	1	x	0	0
4	1	x	1	1

Example − Multiplication

Example:

$0011010 \times 001100 = 100111000$

$$
\begin{array}{r}
0011010 \quad = 26_{10} \\
\times 0001100 \quad = 12_{10} \\
\hline
0000000 \\
0000000 \\
0011010 \\
0011010 \\
\hline
0100111000 \quad = 312_{10}
\end{array}
$$

Binary Division

Binary division is similar to decimal division. It is called as the long division procedure.

Example − Division

101010 / 000110 = 000111

$$
\begin{array}{r}
1\,1\,1 \qquad = 7_{10} \\
000110\,)\overline{1\,0\,1\,0\,1\,0} \qquad = 42_{10} \\
-1\,1\,0 \qquad = 6_{10} \\
\overline{1\,0\,0\,1} \\
-1\,1\,0 \\
\overline{1\,1\,0} \\
-1\,1\,0 \\
\overline{0}
\end{array}
$$

BCD:

The binary coded decimal (BCD) is a type of binary code used to represent a given decimal number in an equivalent binary form. Its main advantage is that it allows easy conversion to decimal digits for printing or display and faster calculations. The most common BCD code is the 8421 BCD code. In this, the BCD equivalent of a decimal number is written by replacing each decimal digit in integer and fractional parts with its four-bit binary equivalent '(or nibble). Here 8, 4, 2 and 1 represent the weights of different bits in the four-bit groups, starting from the (MSB) most significant bit (to extreme left) and proceeding towards the least significant (LSB) bit. This feature makes it a weighted code, whose main characteristic is that each binary digit in the four bit group representing a given decimal digit is assigned a weight, and for each group of four bits, the sum of the weights of those binary digits whose value is 1 is equal to the decimal digit which they represent.

Decimal digit	BCD Code 8421	BCD Code 4221	BCD Code 5421
0	0 0 0 0	0 0 0 0	0 0 0 0
1	0 0 0 1	0 0 0 1	0 0 0 1
2	0 0 1 0	0 0 1 0	0 0 1 0
3	0 0 1 1	0 0 1 1	0 0 1 1
4	0 1 0 0	1 0 0 0	0 1 0 0
5	0 1 0 1	0 0 1 1	
6	0 1 1 0	1 1 0 0	1 0 0 1
7	0 1 1 1	1 1 0 1	1 0 1 0
8	1 0 0 0	1 1 1 0	1 0 1 1
9	1 0 0 1	1 1 1 1	1 1 0 0

For example, if we look at table, we find that the decimal digit 9 when represented in 8421 BCD is 1001. Now the decimal digit assigned to first 1 is 8 and to the second 1 is 1. If we add 8 and 1 we get the required decimal number which is 9. The 4221 BCD and 5421 BCD are other weighted BCD codes shown in table. The numbers 4, 2, 2, 1 in 4221 BCD and 5, 4, 2 and 1 in 5421 BCD represent weights of the relevant bits.

Now let us consider some examples, where we convert the given decimal numbers to BCD.

The 8421 BCD code for 9.2 is 1001.0010.

$$9 \qquad . \qquad 2$$
$$1001 \qquad\qquad 0010$$

The 4221 BCD code for 9.2 is 1111.0010.

The 5421 BCD code for 9.2 is 1100.0010.

BCD code is useful for outputting to displays that are always numeric (0 to 9), such as those found in digital clocks or digital voltmeters.

ASCII:

ASCII Computer Code Computers work in binary code. Information is coded using 0s and 1s. Each 0 or 1 is called a bit. In the early years of computer development, different computer companies applied the binary system in their own way. The code for the letters in the word "cat" was often different in different brands of computers.

Eventually, a set of standards was developed. Computer manufacturers agreed to use one code called the ASCII (American Standard Code for Information Interchange). ASCII is an 8-bit code. That is, it uses eight bits to represent a letter or a punctuation mark. Eight bits are called a byte. A binary code with eight digits, such as 1101 10112, can be stored in one byte of computer memory. The word "CAT" in a word processor becomes 0100 00112, 0100 00012, and 0101 01002. The word "cat" is 0110 00112, 0110 00012, and 0111 01002.

Each letter, number, and symbol are represented by an 8-bit ASCII code. Part of the ASCII code is given in this handout. Notice that there is even an ASCII code for a blank space.

Character	Decimal Number	Binary Number	Character	Decimal Number	Binary Number
blank space	32	0010 0000	^	94	0101 1110
!	33	0010 0001	_	95	0101 1111
"	34	0010 0010	`	96	0110 0000
#	35	0010 0011	a	97	0110 0001
$	36	0010 0100	b	98	0110 0010
A	65	0100 0001	c	99	0110 0011
B	66	0100 0010	d	100	0110 0100
C	67	0100 0011	e	101	0110 0101
D	68	0100 0100	f	102	0110 0110
E	69	0100 0101	g	103	0110 0111
F	70	0100 0110	h	104	0110 1000
G	71	0100 0111	i	105	0110 1001
H	72	0100 1000	j	106	0110 1010
I	73	0100 1001	k	107	0110 1011
J	74	0100 1010	l	108	0110 1100
K	75	0100 1011	m	109	0110 1101
L	76	0100 1100	n	110	0110 1110
M	77	0100 1101	o	111	0110 1111
N	78	0100 1110	p	112	0111 0000
O	79	0100 1111	q	113	0111 0001
P	80	0101 0000	r	114	0111 0010
Q	81	0101 0001	s	115	0111 0011
R	82	0101 0010	t	116	0111 0100
S	83	0101 0011	u	117	0111 0101
T	84	0101 0100	v	118	0111 0110
U	85	0101 0101	w	119	0111 0111
V	86	0101 0110	x	120	0111 1000
W	87	0101 0111	y	121	0111 1001
X	88	0101 1000	z	122	0111 1010
Y	89	0101 1001	{	123	0111 1011
Z	90	0101 1010	|	124	0111 1100
[	91	0101 1011	}	125	0111 1101
/	92	0101 1100	~	126	0111 1110
]	93	0101 1101			

EBCDIC:

The ASCII code discussed above was quickly adopted by the majority of American computer manufacturers, and was eventually turned into an international standard (see also the discussions on ISO and Unicode later in this paper.) However, IBM already had its own six-bit code called BCDIC (Binary Coded Decimal Interchange Code). Thus, IBM decided to go its own way, and it developed a proprietary 8-bit code called the Extended Binary Coded Decimal Interchange Code (EBCDIC). Pronounced "eb-sea-dick" by some and "eb-sid-ick" by others, EBCDIC was first used on the IBM 360 computer, which was presented to the market in 1964. As was noted in our earlier discussions, one of the really nice things about ASCII is that all of the alpha characters are numbered sequentially. In turn, this means that we can perform programming tricks like saying "char = 'A' + 23" and have a reasonable expectation of ending up with the letter 'X'. To cut a long story short, if you were thinking of doing this with EBCDIC ... don't. The reason we say this is apparent from the table shown in Fig.

Fig. EBCDIC character codes.

2nd hex digit \ 1st hex digit	0	1	2	3	4	5	6	7	8	9	A	B	C	D	E	F
0	NUL	DLE	DS		SP	&	-									0
1	SOH	DC1	SOS				/		a	j			A	J		1
2	STX	DC2	FS	SYN					b	k	s		B	K	S	2
3	ETX	TM							c	l	t		C	L	T	3
4	PF	RES	BYP	PN					d	m	u		D	M	U	4
5	HT	NL	LF	RS					e	n	v		E	N	V	5
6	LC	BS	ETB	UC					f	o	w		F	O	W	6
7	DEL	IL	ESC	EOT					g	p	x		G	P	X	7
8		CAN							h	q	y		H	Q	Y	8
9		EM							i	r	z	'	I	R	Z	9
A	SMM	CC	SM		¢ CENT	!		:								
B	VT	CU1	CU2	CU3		$	,	#								
C	FF	IFS		DC4	<	*	%	@								
D	CR	IGS	ENQ	NAK	(	)	_	'								
E	SO	IRS	ACK		+	;	>	=								
F	SI	IUS	BEL	SUB	|	¬	?	"								

A brief glance at this illustration shows just why EBCDIC can be such a pain to use – the alphabetic characters don't have sequential codes. That is, the letters 'A' through 'I' occupy codes $C1 to $C9, 'J' through 'R' occupy codes $D1 to $D9, and 'S' through 'Z' occupy code$E2 to $E9 (and similarly for the lowercase letters). Thus, performing programming tricks such as using the expression ('A' + 23) is somewhat annoying with EBCDIC. Another nuisance is that EBCDIC doesn't contain all of the ASCII codes, which makes transferring text files between the two representations somewhat problematical.

Once again, in addition to the standard alphanumeric characters ('a'...'z', 'A'...'Z' and 0'...'9'), punctuation characters (comma, period, semi-colon, ...), and special characters ('!', '#', '%', ...), EBCDIC includes a lot of strange mnemonics, such as ACK, NAK, and BEL, which were designed for communications purposes. Some of these codes are still used today, while others are, generally speaking, of historical interest only. A slightly more detailed breakdown of these codes is presented in Fig below for your edification and delight.

As one final point of interest, different countries have different character requirements, such as the á, ê, and ü characters. Due to the fact that IBM sold its computer systems around the world, it had to create multiple versions of EBCDIC. In fact, 57 different national variants were eventually wending their way across the planet. (A "standard" with 57 variants! You can only imagine how much fun everybody had when transferring files from one country to another).

ACK	Acknowledge	IGS	Interchange group separator
BEL	Bell	IL	Idle
BS	Backspace	IRS	Interchange record separator
BYP	Bypass	IUS	Interchange unit separator
CAN	Cancel	LC	Lowercase
CC	Cursor control	LF	Line feed
CR	Carriage return	NAK	Negative acknowledge
CU1	Customer use 1	NL	New line
CU2	Customer use 2	NUL	Null
CU3	Customer use 3	PF	Punch off
DC1	Device control 1	PN	Punch on
DC2	Device control 2	RES	Restore
DC4	Device control 4	RS	Reader stop
DEL	Delete	SI	Shift in
DLE	Data link escape	SM	Set mode
DS	Digit select	SMM	Start of manual message
EM	End of medium	SO	Shift out
ENQ	Enquiry	SOH	Start of heading
EOT	End of transmission	SOS	Start of significance
ESC	Escape	SP	Space
ETB	End of transmission block	STX	Start of text
ETX	End of text	SUB	Substitute
FF	Form feed	SYN	Synchronous idle
FS	Field separator	TM	Tape mark
HT (TAB)	Horizontal tab	UC	Uppercase
IFS	Interchange file separator	VT	Vertical tab

Fig. EBCDIC control codes.

UNICODE:

Unicode is an entirely new idea in setting up binary codes for text or script characters. Officially called the Unicode Worldwide Character Standard, it is a system for "the interchange, processing, and display of the written texts of the diverse languages of the modern world." It also supports many classical and historical texts in a number of languages. These characters cover the principal written languages of the world.

Unlike ASCII, which uses 7 bits for each character, Unicode uses 16 bits, which means that it can represent more than 65,000 unique characters. This is a bit of overkill for English and Western-European languages, but it is necessary for some other languages, such as Greek, Chinese and Japanese. Many analysts believe that as the software industry becomes increasingly global, Unicode will eventually supplant ASCII as the standard character coding format.

Gray Code:

The Gray code was designed by Frank Gray at Bell Laboratories and patented in 1953. The Gray code is un-weighted and is not an arithmetic code; that is, there are no weights assigned to the bit positions. The important feature of the Gray code is that it exhibits only a single bit change from one code word to the next in sequence. Owing to this feature, the maximum error that can creep into a system using the binary Gray code to encode data is much less than the worst-case error encountered in the case of straight binary encoding. This property is important in many applications, such as shaft position encoders, where error chance increases with the number of bit changes between adjacent numbers in a sequence. Table here lists the binary and Gray code equivalents of decimal numbers from 0–15.

Decimal	Binary Code (input)	Gray Code (output)
0	0000	0000
1	0001	0001
2	0010	0011
3	0011	0010
4	0100	0110
5	0101	0111
6	0110	0101
7	0111	0100
8	1000	1100
9	1001	1101
10	1010	1111
11	1011	1110
12	1100	1010
13	1101	1011
14	1110	1001
15	1111	1000

Binary numbers are shown in the table for reference. Like binary numbers, the Gray code can have any number of bits. Notice the single-bit change between successive Gray code words. For instance, in going from decimal 3 to decimal 4, the Gray code changes from 0010 to 0110, while the binary code changes from 0011 to 0100, a change of three bits. The only bit change is in the third bit from the right in the Gray code; the others remain the same. An examination of the four-bit Gray code numbers shows that the last entry rolls over to the first entry. That is, the last and the first entry also differ by only 1 bit. This is known as the cyclic property of the Gray code. Although there can be more than one Gray code for a given word length, the term was first applied to a specific binary code for non-negative integers and called the binary-reflected Gray code or simply the Gray code. There are various ways by which Gray codes with a given number of bits can be remembered. One such way is to remember that the least significant bit follows a repetitive pattern of '2' (11, 00, 11 ...), the next higher adjacent bit follows a pattern of '4' (1111, 0000, 1111 ...) and so on.

Logic Gates:

Logic gates are the basic building blocks of any digital system. It is an electronic circuit having one or more than one input and only one output. The relationship between the input and the output is based on a certain logic. Based on this, logic gates are named as AND gate, OR gate, NOT gate etc.

1. **OR Gate:** An OR gate has two or more inputs and a single output and it operates in accordance with the following definition:

    The n inputs to a logic circuit are designated by A, B, . . ., N and the output by Y, it is to be understood that each of these symbols may assume one of two possible values, either 0 or 1. The standard electronic symbol for the OR gate is in fig below together with the Boolean expression for this gate.

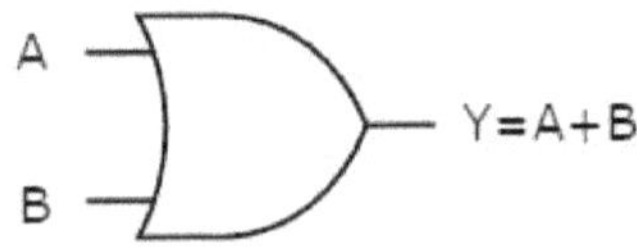

$$Y = A + B$$

The OR gate represents the Boolean equation

$$A + B = Y$$

Truth Table for OR-gate

Input		Output
A	**B**	**Y**
0	0	0
0	1	1
1	0	1
1	1	1

2. **AND gate:** An AND gate has two or more inputs and a single output, and it operates in accordance with the following definition, the output of an and assumes the 1state if and only if all the inputs assume the 1 state.

The n inputs to a logic circuit will be designated by A, B, . . . N and the output by Y, and each of these symbols may assume one of two possible values, either 0 or 1. The standard symbol for the AND circuit is given in fig.

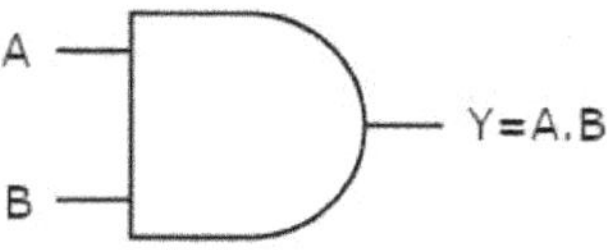

$$Y = A + B$$

The Boolean expression of N-inputs AND gate is

$$Y = A.B.C......N$$

The Truth Table for AND gate is

Input		Output
A	**B**	**Y**
0	0	0
0	1	0
1	0	0
1	1	1

3. **NOT gate:** A NOT gate, often called an inverter, is a nice digital logic gate to start with because it has only a single input with simple behavior. A NOT gate performs logical negation on its input. In other words, if the input is 1, then the output will be 0. Similarly, a 0 input results in a 1 output.

The symbol for NOT gate is

The Truth Table for NOT gate is

Input	Output
A	B
0	1
1	0

4. **NAND gate:** A NAND Gate is a logical gate which is the opposite of an AND logic gate. It is a combination of AND and NOT gates and is a commonly used logic gate. It is considered as a "universal" gate in Boolean algebra as it is capable of producing all other logic gates.

The symbol for NAND gate is

The Truth table for NAND gate is

Input		Output
A	B	Y
0	0	1
0	1	1
1	0	1
1	1	0

5. **NOR gate:** A NOR gate (sometimes referred to by its extended name, Negated OR gate) is a digital logic gate with two or more inputs and one output with behavior

that is the opposite of an OR gate. The output of a NOR gate is 1 if all of its inputs are 0. If one or more of a NOR gate's inputs are 1, then the output of the NOR gate is 0.

The Symbol for NOR gate is

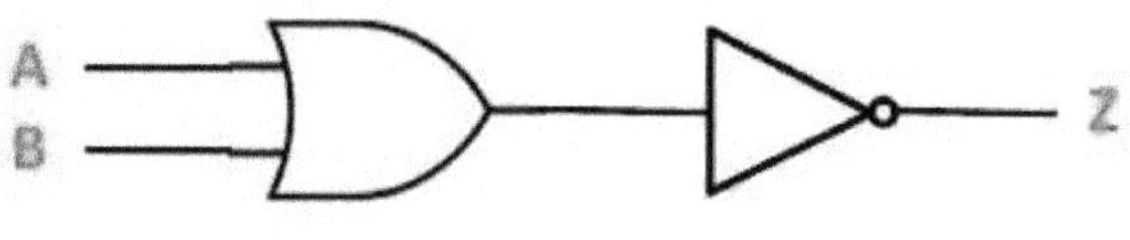

The truth table for NOR gate is

Input		Output
A	B	Y
0	0	1
0	1	0
1	0	0
1	1	0